BOOSTING YOU

The Book That Helps YOU Become a More
Successful Executive

Elias Aractingi
www.boostingyou.com

ISBN 978-0-615-50314-1

Production Assistance: Hala Al-Sayed, Aline and Paul Bajanian

Photos by Andrea Aractingi

2

To all my heroes, who helped shape my life, many of whom appear in name or in alias in the following pages.

4

CONTENTS

Prologue

My career in business has spanned more than 25 years. Over these years, I have had the opportunity to restructure many institutions in the USA, the Far East and the Middle East. I have worked as a management consultant and as a business executive, and in both roles I have had the chance to develop hundreds of successful executives and offer them a chance to improve themselves. I can say confidently that I have not met any company or person who couldn't improve with my help.

Many recipes for success are basic and widely known: be positive, work hard, listen to your customers, learn from your failures, motivate your team, etc. In my experience working to improve corporations and managers, including myself, I have come across a number of concepts that are not part of the current managerial improvement culture even though they present major improvement potential. In recent years, I have come to realize that these concepts are the major reason I have been able to help people (and help myself) succeed, precisely because they are off the beaten path and are even sometimes counterintuitive.

So, I have decided to write this book to share these concepts with executives and would-be executives in businesses large and small to help lift their performance.

I have structured this book in the form of an improvement plan. You should approach it with an open mind and use it to detect areas of your own performance that you can improve.

In your business life, there are three major components:
- The first component is you. It is the first thing we need to work on before tackling anything else. I am a strong believer in the theory that your best friend is you, and your biggest enemy is also you. So the first area of improvement has to be making you aware of certain tricks you are playing against yourself and reinforcing your belief in you.
- The second component is your team. The people who work for you, whose success is dependent on your success and who make your success a reality. These are

the people who leverage your skills and whose skills you leverage. The next area of improvement deals with finding these people and getting them to reach their full potential.

- The third component is your customers. You have internal and external customers. Your internal customers are your bosses. Your external customers are people and institutions to whom your institution sells products and services. The final area of improvement deals with the value you provide to your internal and external customers and how to maximize it.

A final note before we proceed: This book is simple and straightforward, the way my approach to people and organizations has always been.

So, without further ado, let's start with our first step: exploring YOU.

YOU

Introduction: How You Can Improve YOU

This is November 2008. The tennis Davis Cup Final has just ended. It pitched the team from Argentina against the team from Spain. The format of the Davis Cup is 5 matches: 4 singles and 1 doubles, and the winning team is the one that has 3 or more wins in these 5 matches. Normally, Spain would have been a favorite because Spaniard Rafael Nadal was then the best player in the world, meaning that he would very likely win 2 singles matches and possibly even be part of the doubles team, making a doubles win likely as well for a total of 3 matches. Except that this time, Nadal couldn't participate, being on recovery for an injury. Because of Nadal's absence, the Argentines became the favorites: Argentina's top two players, Juan Martin del Potro, ranked 9th in the world, and David Nalbandian, the world number 11, were both expected to win their two singles matches against lower ranked Spaniards, giving Argentina 4 wins (and the crown, since 3 wins are enough). Making matters better for the Argentines, the matches were to be played in Argentina, giving the local team the home turf advantage, a time-proven motivational boost. Compounding this advantage, the Argentines decided to play on a fast surface, which suits their players better since the Spaniards are known for their slow-court expertise. So what happened?

The first match went Argentina's way, as expected, as Nalbandian, the second-best Argentine player, quickly dismissed David Ferrer, the top Spaniard, thus giving Argentina a 1-0 lead. The next match, which should have been a walk in the park for Argentina, saw the demise of Argentina's top-ranked player del Potro against Spain's Feliciano Lopez, the world number 30. That loss by del Potro was the catalyst that precipitated Spain's upset over Argentina: the next day, Argentina's doubles team lost to Spain's. The day after, the Argentines decided not to let del Potro, who was depicted as very tired, play. They replaced him with Jose Asacuso, the world number 48, who was no match for Spain's Fernando Verdasco, ranked 16th in the world.

Let's focus on the loss of favorite del Potro to underdog Lopez. Why is that relevant to you? Because one part of improving you is to make sure you win the battles you are supposed to win, unlike del Potro. The other part of improving you is to help you win some of the battles you were expected to lose, as Lopez did.

The first two chapters of the YOU section of the book are dedicated to making sure you have what it takes to fulfill your ambitions:

- The first deals with defeating the enemy within you to make sure you are only fighting against the outside world, not fighting against yourself and the outside world
- The second chapter is concerned with increasing your inner strength so you can operate at levels of performance exceeding your current best.

After having finished chapters one and two, you should be in good general shape. Chapters three and four provide you with some tools to further improve yourself before you face the outside world.

In the workplace, you will be confronted with two enemies and each chapter focuses on one kind of enemy:

- The first enemy you will meet is the unknown! Knowing that there are things you don't know and cannot control can be very stressful. Chapter 3 will provide you with a framework to confront the unknown while keeping your sanity.
- The next enemy is everyone else! Not everyone around you shares your agenda or your goals, and even if they did, many people around you have self-destructive tendencies and escape issues. You could be drawn into countless side battles that will only distract you from your main priorities. Chapter 4, called "Focus", will discuss how to concentrate your energy to achieve better results.

Having completed the first four chapters, you should be in a position to function at almost 100% of your long-term capacity. That is probably much better than 90% of executives around you. The next two chapters will introduce advanced concepts that will show you how to function at many multiples of your current capacity, by making you aware of new sources of energy:

12

- Chapter 5 discusses emotions and transactions and introduces the concept of using emotions as a source of energy.
- Chapter 6 discusses the setbacks you are likely to encounter within your career and how to use these setbacks as a springboard to a better future.

Chapter 1: Aligning YOU

French psychologist/philosopher Pierre Janet, who practiced in the late 1800s/early 1900s, was the first person to coin the words "subconscious mind". The subconscious mind, defined as the portion of our mind that is beyond our consciousness, has fascinated many psychologists, yogis, philosophers and gurus. A quick search on Google or on YouTube will yield a lot of interesting material on the topic. Everyone seems to agree that the subconscious mind is by many orders of magnitude more powerful than the conscious mind.

From there, most gurus focus on harnessing the power of the subconscious mind, which is in effect moving the power of the subconscious into the conscious. That is not the focus of this chapter: our more limited ambition is to align conscious and subconscious, in effect ensuring that your subconscious mind is not fighting against you.

I have had my own personal encounters with the subconscious, which I would like to share with you.

I was about 15 when a group of European magicians gave a Magic Show at the Casino du Liban. I was too young to attend, but my parents did as well as most of their friends. That show was probably the most entertaining to take place in Lebanon in that era. For many weeks after it, the social circles in Beirut had only one subject of conversation, and that was the show. It was later broadcast on TV, where I saw it, and everyone I know stayed home to watch it. The highlight of the show was a hypnotist -to this day, I remember his name: Yvon Yva- who asked more than 20 persons from the audience to go on stage and then proceeded to hypnotize them all and then suggest to them that they were hot, they were cold, they were hungry, etc., to the delight of the audience who was watching their reactions.

The episode piqued me enough that, a few months later, I picked up a small pocket book from a collection of "how to" French books about hypnosis. After reading the book, I developed a rudimentary technique to hypnotize people and began testing it on anybody around me who would

14

volunteer. Most people would resist, but I had a cousin who was a very good subject. So, with another cousin who acted as my assistant, I began to hold hypnosis sessions starring my cousin Yasmina. At first, we limited ourselves to the "you're hot, you're cold" type of suggestions. With time, however, Yasmina began to fall in a trance much faster, and to talk while in a trance, responding to questions, offering insights, etc.

Yasmina was only 14 at the time, so these conversations were not very profound. What was intriguing, though, was that she was saying things that were completely at odds with the opinions she usually expressed when conscious: the people she loved, the events that marked her, her personal fears, etc., were not the same in her conscious mind as what her unconscious mind revealed through hypnosis. For example, she could profess her undying friendship for someone in her conscious mind and reveal, under hypnosis, that she didn't like that person. To such an extent that she often wanted us to hypnotize her so we could share with her her subconscious insights afterwards.

By way of anecdote, let me mention that Yasmina is now a world-renowned psychic, based in London. I am sure that the ease with which she is able to access her subconscious played a key role in her success as a psychic.

The experience with Yasmina created in me, at a very early age, an awareness of the subconscious. It dawned on me that we are really composed of two parts, one conscious and the other subconscious. Still, I never felt that it affected me in any way. I viewed myself as a very uncomplicated person and never thought my own subconscious could trick me or behave in ways outside my control. It is only much later, also through first-hand experience, that I became aware that I too had a subconscious mind living within me that had its own opinions and behaviors.

I was about 32 and happily married. I had been stationed in Jakarta, Indonesia, working on a bank restructuring assignment, and my wife was in New York, living with her parents: She was about to deliver our first baby and had gone back to New York for that purpose. My assignment was scheduled to end around the time the baby was due, and I was scheduled to go to New York, attend the delivery, then spend a few days with my wife and the new baby before starting a new assignment, this time in Jeddah, Saudi Arabia. As it happened, my wife delivered a few days early, so I became the proud father of a beautiful baby girl while still in Jakarta. A few days later, I joined my wife at her parents' house in Queens, New York.

I would usually spend my days holding the new baby. At night, my wife I and would retire to our room, in which a crib was installed for the baby. Like all babies, ours would wake up several times a night and start crying. Now there are two schools of thought as to what one should do in such cases: The first contends that you should try to impose a certain discipline on the baby, feeding her at specific times and not always responding to her waking up. The second holds that you need to respond to every cry by the baby, lest she feels abandoned and grows up with emotional scars. I was a strong proponent of the first approach, having experienced it myself as a baby with no emotional scars I was aware of. My wife agreed with me. It is fair to say that my mother-in-law was a proponent of the second approach.

My mother-in-law had a great love for the new baby and was really devoted to her. Since I was in Indonesia, she was the one to attend Lamasz classes with my wife and she had even attended the delivery. So, at night, when the baby began to cry and I urged my wife to be patient and let the baby cry a little, my mother-in-law would storm into the room, take the baby and cajole her, often feeding her outside the schedule. I obviously resented this intrusion into our bedroom, but kept my anger inside, since I knew my mother-in-law was not doing this out of malice, but out of love.

One morning, as I was getting dressed, I couldn't find my watch. I looked for it inside the room but couldn't find it. I searched for it very thoroughly, looking under the crib several times. I started complaining to my wife that I had lost the watch, probably because her mother kept barging inside the room. Upon sensing the tension, my mother-in-law came in and asked what was going on, so I told her I couldn't find the watch. She searched the room very quickly, then lifted the crib... and showed me the watch smack under it! I was flabbergasted! This was a very evident place and I had looked there at least 5 times!

So how is it possible for my eyes to have been looking at something without seeing it? It was as if you were looking at a wall with a shelf on it and you only saw a blank wall! For the first time in my life, I realized my subconscious mind could play tricks on me! I reflected on the incident and decided that my subconscious was sending me a message that I was being unfair to my mother-in-law. From that moment on, I became extremely supportive of her.

So if you agree with me that each one of us has a subconscious part that can make him not see something in front of his eyes, it is not difficult to agree that this subconscious part can:

- Make him lose a tennis match, say the wrong things at an interview, get sick just before a major event, be over-combative at work and take up self-destructive behavior such as overdrinking

- Or, to the contrary, rise up to the occasion and win the tennis match of a lifetime, make the right split-second decisions and deliver consistent performance.

How powerful is your subconscious? Most knowledgeable sources will tell you that it is by orders of magnitude more powerful than your conscious intellect, but we have no way of knowing. I personally believe it is so powerful, it acts sometimes as your guardian angel, and could be confused with a paranormal phenomenon. For example, I believe that some miracles are actually manifestations of the subconscious.

Let me illustrate this with another incident that happened to me. I was about 20 and was in my senior college year. I was beginning the MBA applications process, concentrating on the most prestigious graduate schools. At that time, the selection process focused on three criteria: your academic record, your GMAT score and your work experience after college. I had an excellent academic record but I wasn't planning to spend more than one year working between college and graduate school, so I needed an outstanding GMAT score to be considered at the schools I wanted. Since I usually did very well at standardized tests (and being very cocky at the time), I decided I didn't need to prepare for the GMAT. That was very dangerous because graduate schools at that time always took into consideration your first test score if you took the test more than once.

The day before I was scheduled to take the test, I had a very severe flu, and the day of the test I was in bed with very high fever. So I didn't take the test. When I went to the registration center to register for another test, I saw a brochure advertising a GMAT textbook. I took it and started looking at it: on the back were some sample test questions, so I tried to resolve them. To my big surprise, all my answers were incorrect: clearly, there were parts of the test with a logic that was entirely foreign to me. So, I bought the book and spent a month prior to the rescheduled test date training with the book. I had a great score and got into Columbia.

Put simply, my sudden flu had saved me from a mediocre score, which would probably have killed my graduate school chances. Three factors can possibly explain this beneficial flu:

- It could be pure luck.

- It could be destiny, or the Hand of a Greater Power.

- It could be my subconscious mind.

Given that I have a tendency to catch the flu at convenient moments in life (for example, after I have finished exams, never before a big date or interview, etc.), I would give at least a 50% probability to the third possibility, the subconscious.

So, let us pause here and agree on the following:

- There is such a thing as your subconscious mind.

- It could help you or possibly play tricks on you.

- It is very powerful, much more powerful than your conscious mind.

If you agree to all of the above, what do you do?

I suggest that you start by what you don't do. What you don't do is coerce your subconscious mind to behave as you would like it to behave. Why? a. Because it is stronger than you are and b. because it is smarter than you are. To recap, imagine two brothers, one of whom is driving a car and the other being the passenger. The passenger is much smarter and much stronger than the driver. If the passenger wants to go somewhere and the driver wants to go somewhere else, there is a problem. The driver will have a very hard time imposing his views on the much stronger passenger. In addition, it makes sense for the driver to listen to the passenger and understand why this much smarter individual

18

wants to go somewhere else. Maybe it is their common interest to go to that other place. So, the smart thing to do is for the two brothers to have a discussion and for the driver to be completely open to his brother's views. If they agree, not only will the passenger not hinder the driving but he will also help and provide directions and insights that will make the journey shorter!

So, the right thing to do is to have an open discussion with your subconscious mind. How do you do that?

The first step is to listen to the subconscious mind's messages. These can come to you:

- During sleep: Are your dreams predictable? Do you dream while asleep pretty much the same dreams as when you're awake? Are your nightmares similar to your daily worries? If so, congratulations: your subconscious mind is on your side! But for maybe 90% of the population, that's not the case. An extreme example would be a friend's son who sometimes dreamt he was being choked by an unknown assailant and would wake up deeply disturbed in the middle of the night. Another example is a colleague who always had the same nightmare; he was run over by a car.

- During the day: Look for any behavior of yours that one would describe as abnormal. For example, a business acquaintance who used to stress so much his entire body would become numb; he consulted all kinds of cardiologists who couldn't seem to find anything wrong with him. A relative gets intense anxiety attacks any time he needs to travel. Another relative becomes so impatient with her staff that she regularly has nerve-wrecking anger attacks; she is unable to hold a job for more than six months. All these symptoms could be physical, so by all means see a psychiatrist if you have them, while also allowing that they could be messages from your subconscious mind.

- More subtle hints: Do you sometimes say the wrong things just before closing a major deal? Do you fail tests that you should ace? Do you have difficulty to concentrate on a specific subject or with a specific individual and not with others? Do you often make stupid calculation errors on important documents? Do you often leave blaring typos on important letters? Do you often quarrel with your peers when a more humble approach would get you what you want? Do you take unnecessary risks at work? Is your behavior with coworkers of the other gender close to sexual harassment? Do you lie when telling the truth wouldn't harm you? Are you overly forgetful? Do you lose stuff too often? Do you smoke or drink a little more than you should?

By sending you these messages or even sabotaging your efforts, your subconscious mind could be:

- Either giving you some practical, tactical help, as in: you are not ready to take the quiz now, so I'll make you sick today but please study next time.

- Or disagreeing with your overall objectives, as in: you are not ready to take this promotion and if you do, you'll bomb, so I'm going to make sure your boss doesn't promote you. That way, you'll remain in your comfort zone, which is better for you long-term.

Let us look back at the fateful tennis match between Argentine player Juan Martin del Potro and Spain's Feliciano Lopez. Recall that this is the match that arguably lost Argentina its hope of earning its first Davis Cup. Now, let us assume that the higher-ranked del Potro, playing on the surface of his choice and encouraged by his own crowd, was sabotaged by his subconscious mind. Let us now, on behalf of del Potro, ask his subconscious mind why he made him lose:

- One possible answer could be tactical: My dear Juan Martin, you were physically stretched, having just come back from China and the Masters. I wanted to keep you in shape for the Australian Open a couple of months down the road and I wanted to make sure you didn't get some kind of long-term injury.

- The more likely answer would be strategic: My dear Juan Martin, you started the year at lower than number 50 worldwide and you are now number 9. You are only 20 now. A successful match, and the first Davis Cup ever for your country, would propel you to almost godlike heights and I am not sure you can take the sudden pressure of success. I'd rather teach you the meaning of humility now and plan for a long-term career in which you might win a Davis Cup in the future, believe me you'll be very motivated and you'll have another chance! I have seen too many athletes burn out early to take the chance of letting you win!

After this conversation with his subconscious mind, del Potro would start to work on his humility, his consistency and his maturity to earn the confidence of his subconscious mind. If he does that, expect to see him at the top of the tennis circuit in the next few years. In our definition, he will have achieved alignment with his subconscious mind, with both of them working in tandem.

20

That's my ambition for you: achieving alignment. To do that, you need to be in touch with your subconscious mind and able to evaluate yourself objectively:

- Are you working in the field that is best adapted to your competences, interest and personality? Or are you in your profession because of peer pressure, prestige or money?

- If you are lobbying for a promotion, are you competent enough to assume the added responsibilities? Are you the best person for the job?

- If you succeed in whatever you are working on, will you be able to handle the success? Will you be happier or less happy as a result of that success and your changed lifestyle?

If the answer to any of those questions is no, congratulations! You have begun the dialogue with your subconscious mind. Now you can start addressing the issues that cause your conflict:

- This may involve changing career paths: I personally found being a manager more attuned to my personality than being a consultant, and being a consultant more self-rewarding than being a private banker.

- Or it may involve more training, reading, learning, until you acquire the conviction that you (a) deserve that promotion and (b) you're uniquely qualified for the new job.

- In any case, it will involve reviewing your priorities, your commitments and your desired lifestyle to see how they fit with the goals you are pursuing.

At the end of the road, you will be aligned: self-confident, clear, consistent and ready for achievement.

****
Aligning YOU and Religion

We have discussed in chapter one the power of the subconscious mind and touched on its capacity to accomplish paranormal things. We have also touched on the therapeutic benefits of self-alignment. Many people have achieved similar results through religion. From there, the following issues merit consideration:

- Is God present within us or completely outside us?

- Is the act of praying an outward event or an inward act: In other words, do we pray in order to ask something from an outside entity (God, a saint, a prophet, a dead relative, etc.) or to get our internal self at peace and focused on a specific goal, such as with meditation? Or a mixture of both?

For the answer to these questions, I have conducted a limited research in the teachings of the four major religions.

The oldest of these four major religions, Buddhism, is the one that most strongly preaches inward peace and melds prayer and meditation. The following quote from the book "The Last Teaching of the Buddha" as published by Bukkyo Dendo Kyokai (Society for the Promotion of Buddhism) is self-explanatory: "The point of the teachings is to control your own mind. Keep your mind from greed, and you will keep your behavior right, your mind pure and your words faithful. By always thinking about the transience of your life, you will be able to resist greed and anger, and will be able to avoid all evils. If you find your mind tempted and so entangled in greed, you must suppress and control the temptation; be the master of your own mind. A man's mind makes him a Buddha, or it may make him a beast. Misled by error, one becomes a demon; enlightened, one becomes a Buddha. Therefore, control your mind and do not let it deviate from the right path." We will note from this passage the primacy of mindset over behavior, as in "have the right mind" versus "do or don't do this or that". We will also note the presence of the Divine within our own self through our ability to become a Buddha.

From Buddhism to Christianity, my native religion: I have read the four Gospels, searching for Christianity's position concerning these issues.

22

While Christianity is clearly concerned with behavior, it also attaches great importance to the mind:

- "Blessed are the pure at heart, for they shall see God" (Matthew 5,8)

- "A good man out of the good treasure of his heart brings forth good; and an evil man out of the evil treasure of his heart brings forth evil. For out of the abundance of the heart his mouth speaks" (Luke 7,45)

Christianity allows for the possibility of demons taking hold of our inner self and there are a number of passages referring to people possessed by demons, such as "Now when He rose early on the first day of the week, He appeared first to Mary Magdalene, out of whom He had cast seven demons" (Mark 16,9)

So if demons can reside in us, so can the Divine. References to that can also be found in the Gospels:

- "And He took bread, gave thanks and broke it, and gave it to them, saying, 'This is My body which is given for you; do this in remembrance of Me.'" (Luke 22,19)

- "At that day, you will know that I am in My Father, and you in Me, and I in you" (John 14, 20)

- "These things I have spoken to you, that My joy may remain in you, and that your joy may be full" (John 15,11)

For both Judaism and Islam, one must be more creative to see evidence of the inner divine. Both religions reckon that Adam, the first man, was created with earth's mud but his soul came about through God's breath. So if God's breath is the origin of our souls, it is not too far fetched to see a piece of God in us.

Interestingly, both Judaism and Islam offer many opportunities for introspection:

- In Judaism, the Shabbat, the day of rest is sacred. It is forbidden to conduct any work on that day, which is exclusively reserved for rest and prayer.

- In Islam, a number of measures are designed to break the daily routine and open the soul to reflection: one must pray 5 times a day at specific times, one must fast during the Holy month of Ramadan and one must perform the Hajj, or Holy Pilgrimage at least once in a lifetime.

I think it is clear that all major religions recognize directly or indirectly the power of our inner self and provide avenues for their adherents to be in touch with it. Whether you are deeply religious or agnostic, I believe you cannot achieve your best without harnessing that power.

****

Chapter 2: Strengthening YOU

This chapter focuses on building your inner strength.

Consider this: the more you like and admire a person, the more you are willing to do things for her. Many people in the USA have provided countless hours of their time and work for free as volunteers for one of the presidential candidates. Many people are willing to wait for hours to catch a glimpse of Madonna getting out of her hotel when she visits a given city. Imagine you admiring yourself so much that you can get your conscious and subconscious mind to harness this incredible energy toward achieving your goals!

What makes you admire somebody? Make a test for yourself: take five minutes and write down the names of people you admire, and then the reasons you admire them. You will likely reach the following conclusions:

- You admire people who do good things for others.
- You admire people who have a strong, credible moral code and who are ethically uncompromising.
- You admire people who are extraordinarily gifted in an area you consider important.
- You admire people who help you achieve your goals and give to you in a selfless manner.
-

Since our goal is to help you admire your own self, we will focus on the first three items and help you build a self that is admirable.

The first component you should be looking at is building a **sense of achievement**. This requires evaluating how what you are doing benefits society and being comfortable with the answer:

- In my two years as private banker, I used to agonize over how working on convincing wealthy individuals to bring their assets from undeveloped countries such as Mexico into Switzerland or the USA was beneficial for society as a whole. I resolved my conflict by persuading myself that offering these people an outlet for their surpluses in a developed country would increase their motivation to invest and make profits in their home country. Plus, part of their capital would be protected from devaluation, confiscation, etc., which would make it available for reinvestment in the home country after a crisis. So, while

I did find an ethical purpose for my line of work, it was not very evident or straightforward. Plus, I didn't feel that working as a private banker was where my specific skills would best serve society. My performance, while good, was not stellar and BSI was reducing its presence in New York, so I left.

- In my later career as a management consultant, I struggled with the concept of how reengineering a company, which could result in painful layoffs, was actually something good for society: that was not as difficult. Companies with bureaucracy and inefficiencies gradually lose market share to the point that they become marginally profitable and, if they are able to keep all their employees, these employees receive few raises, incentives and bonuses and are generally demotivated. In addition, there is no room for recruitment, which means no job opportunities for newcomers and no room to grow for the good performers. On the other hand, companies that restructure themselves and become efficient eventually gain market share, enter new businesses and grow their overall employee base. However, while very convinced that restructuring, including downsizing, is actually good, I still prefer working on the revenue generating side of the equation such as business expansion, geographical expansion, etc.

Whatever your profession or field, you should be a person who is adding value to your environment. You need to understand the value you are adding and build a story, such as the two stories above, about how your work is contributing to making this a better world.

Prostitution is vilified by most religions and many parts of society as degrading to women and to love. Yet many prostitutes are really proud of their jobs and view themselves as providers of relaxation services to segments of society that would otherwise be unable to access this relaxation. Alcohol consumption is forbidden by Islam and by the Mormon Church and frowned upon by many people. Yet most bar and liquor store owners see themselves as providers of escape and entertainment to people whose lives would otherwise be boring. The fast food industry is described by many people as wasteful, obesity-promoting and health-destroying. To many proud workers of that industry, it is

26

rather a promoter of consistent standards, inexpensive quality meals, unforgettable children outings and familiar places to visit when on faraway trips. Most people view making cars positively, yet there are many who view the car industry as a conduit for depleting earth's resources and for encouraging conspicuous consumption. A friend of mine has a rule that she will never replace a car that is less than 10 years old and will never buy a car with an engine larger than 1.4 liters. The point is that many occupations have debatable value: the important thing is not how your neighbor, or your friends or your community view your occupation but how you view it. The important thing is for you to believe very strongly in your story so that it becomes a mission.

Another aspect you need to take into consideration is the extent to which the occupation you are currently holding fits with your abilities and potential. You might be working in a soup kitchen, which is something undoubtedly great for humanity. However, if you have the potential to be Albert Einstein, working in a soup kitchen would not be the best use of your time and talent and humanity would be better served with you doing something else!

You should also be doing something that you enjoy doing, so you can do it well and for a long time. Again, working in a soup kitchen is great, but not if it bores you or depresses you.

The second component you should be looking at is building a **coherent moral code** that you can live with and abide by. In military strategy, holding a high position gives you an advantage: the army that occupies the high hills has a distinct advantage over the enemy that is located underneath and has to direct its firepower upward. That could be the origin of the expression "holding the moral high grounds", which is often heard in business situations, and is used to convey that one party has the advantage of being right from a moral perspective.

Being always on the right side of the moral dimension is a source of strength that you should be looking to develop. The moral standards we are looking for don't have to be religious standards; they are ethical standards that should be agreed to by two major parties:

(1) The first and foremost party that should be convinced by your moral code is you. No matter what religion you were raised into or what rules you followed growing up, you need to develop your own sense of right and wrong.

(2) The second party that needs to accept or at least tolerate your moral code is your environment: your coworkers, your society, and your employer. For example, your moral code cannot break the law. It cannot shock the people around you.

As far as I am concerned, I have decided that the following rules apply to any employment I am involved in:

- Principles are the first priority and take precedence over my own interests as well as the interests of the institution I am working for. For example, if my employer is trying to win a major contract in a foreign country and if I would need to bribe certain officials of that country in order to win the contract, I will refuse to do so, even if it means losing the contract.
- My employer's interests come as the next priority, before my own. For example, if I am considered for a promotion and there is a more suitable candidate for it, I would prefer that the best candidate take the job, even if it means a slowdown for me in my career.
- I think of myself last. After all, if I am doing my honest best to further the interests of my employer and I have strong ethical principles, my career should take care of itself.

The third and final area you should be looking to build, as part of strengthening YOU is the relevant **skills** needed to accomplish your work. As CEO of conglomerate GE, Jack Welch, arguably the best CEO of all times, famously said: "We will be number one or two in every business we're in, or we will fix it, close it or sell it". If this objective makes sense for institutions and companies, it makes even more sense for individuals: you don't want to be in a job where the best you can be is second-rate; it is not good for your morale and not good for your future. You want to be in a job where, with the proper mix of training, hard work and experience, you can reach world-class levels of performance.

There may be occupations for which you are not suitable and in which no amount of training or experience will move you to world-class standards. Chances are, however, these don't include your current occupation! When Jack Welch made his famous quote, he didn't intend for it to be the catalyst for a major business exodus by GE; on the contrary, he had faith that he would be able to raise the performance of all his businesses to become leaders. If you are already within a certain job, it is most likely that you have an affinity with that job and much less likely that you are structurally incapable of becoming brilliant at that job.

Let's do another small mental exercise: imagine two young men, both of whom are 18 years old. The first one, who we will name Tiny, is 5'5" (1.65m) and 140 lbs (64 kgs). The second one, who we will name Biggy, is 6'6" (1.95m) and 200 lbs (91 kgs). Now suppose that you are going to meet a person who might want to hurt you, so you need a bodyguard. Who will you choose? Probably Biggy!

Now let's fast-forward 3 years into the future: in those 3 years, Tiny has enrolled in a gym and exercised 15 hours a week. In addition, he has taken Tae Kwon Do classes and reached the level of black belt. During that same period, Biggy has continued his normal practice of playing basketball once a week. Now, if I ask you the same question as before, you may still choose Biggy, on the grounds that he still looks more threatening than Tiny, so your enemy will be deterred by his mere presence! So I'll ask you a slightly different question: you have to select your bodyguard between Tiny and Biggy and whichever person you did not select will be your enemy's bodyguard. Now it looks much more probable that you will select Tiny!

Presumably, you have selected Tiny because you don't want to take the risk of being on the wrong side of a Tae Kwon Do champion! This small exercise in imagination shows us that the training/experience element can account for much more of your skillset than your natural ability.

Let's pursue this imagination drill a bit further and imagine the actual meeting between you, accompanied by Tiny, and your archenemy (let's call him Brutus), with his bodyguard Biggy: Within seconds of the meeting, Brutus begins to threaten you and starts moving toward you. Immediately, Tiny puts himself in front of you and asks Brutus, in a polite but firm manner, to step back. Brutus is a bit annoyed by this intervention and asks Biggy to take care of the problem. Biggy then advances toward Tiny menacingly. Tiny asks Biggy, softly but firmly, to withdraw, and makes a small advance toward him. Biggy is puzzled. Since he is not stupid, he is thinking: "Normally, this small man should be afraid of me and run away. However, he is clearly unafraid of me, and he is a bodyguard, so there must be more to him than meets the eye. I can test him and end up in a hospital if he turns out to be a karate champion, or I can take my client and leave. Let me take the second choice; after all, I am not a professional fighter!"

The second lesson we take from this imagination exercise is that, when you are skilled, you project an aura of confidence that others can perceive, even if you don't use your skills.

Since this exercise is fertile in terms of lessons, let us push it a bit further and now imagine that your enemy, Brutus, had foreseen you would bring a bodyguard with you, and brought, in addition to Biggy, a fighter named Johnny, who was brought up in the Bronx, in a gang, and who learned in jail a version of Kung Fu that does not include the ordinary civilities this fine sport preaches. Johnny is technically very gifted in the art of fighting and does not practice self-restraint. So, Johnny moves Biggy aside and attacks Tiny! What follows is a fierce battle pitting the two athletes, which you are following nervously since you know that if Tiny loses, it's your turn to face the music! Even as Tiny stands his grounds, he is taking a few punches. What is really surprising is that he looks as if he is enjoying himself, although he is receiving some heavy blows! Johnny is also getting hammered and is surprisingly also appearing to have a good time. You, on the other hand, are beginning to worry about the outcome of this confrontation when, thankfully, the police steps in and arrests all involved. When that happens, you are also bewildered to see that Tiny and Johnny are looking at each other affectionately!

On the way to the police station, you are seated next to Tiny, which allows you to ask him the questions that are on your mind: "You must have been worried, Tiny!" Tiny is in a talkative mood: "Yeah, the guy is a good fighter. Had some nice moves!" The conversation keeps going:

- "But I saw you smiling, even as Johnny was hitting you with some serious punches!"
- "Yeah, I'll admit I was enjoying myself. You know my Tae Kwon Do education was mostly club-oriented, where we follow certain gentleman rules. This guy learned Kung Fu in jail, so his fighting isn't so clean."
- "And why should that make you happy?"

30

- "What makes me happy is having a chance to test my skills in the real world. I was really glad that I wasn't doing so bad. Plus, I learned a few moves from the guy!"
- "At the end of the fight, you guys looked at each other as if you were friends, not people who almost killed each other!"
- "It's weird, I'll give you that. But I have to respect someone who obviously trained very hard to fight like that. And he must have been impressed with my Tae Kwon Do, so I'm sure he had respect for me as well!"
- "Do you really believe that beasts like Johnny deserve respect?"
- "Sure, to get to this level of fighting, he must have worked really hard. So, whatever else he has done, at least on this count he gets my vote!"

This imaginary episode is rich in lessons. Let's quickly summarize them:

- Training (or reading or getting coaching) can transform you from a weakling to a heavyweight in your field.
- This transformation will also increase your self-confidence. People around you will perceive this self-confidence.
- You will also enjoy your work more, see small defeats as opportunities to learn more and earn the respect of your (competent) enemies.

So, to recap, strengthening YOU involves three major steps:

- Building a sense of achievement and pride in that what you are doing is beneficial for society at large.
- Building a coherent set of principles that you believe in and that will be accepted and respected by coworkers and customers.
- Strengthening your skillset through training, reading and seeking feedback.

```
**************************************************************
```

Strengthening YOU: Getting the Basics Right

Strengthening YOU is a little bit like turbocharging the engine of your car in preparation for a race: it will definitely help you race faster, but it will also show major limitations if there are things wrong with other parts of your car: If you have a flat tire for example, it is of no use boosting your engine. Or if you don't have seat belts, it could be very dangerous for you to even drive the car.

We all tend to believe we're perfect or at least that our drawbacks are not so bad. I have met many people who had the following issues, but were otherwise great individuals:

- Very poor taste in clothes
- Unkempt appearance, hair
- Strong body odor
- Regular use of inappropriate language
- Inability to ever return phone calls
- Inability to keep deadlines
- Inability to show up on time
- Inability to listen
- Excessive phone interruptions
- Kleptomania

This is not an exhaustive list, but you get the picture! Most of these issues are easily treatable; you owe it to yourself to make sure you don't have them, and if you do, you should take care of them.

If you are serious about strengthening YOU, you should also make sure you are providing yourself with the proper care. Again, not an exhaustive list, but you will get the picture:

- You need to eat reasonably and follow a balanced diet
- You need to walk or do light exercise on a daily basis
- You need to get enough sleep
- You should not consume an inordinate amount of tobacco or alcohol
- You should fight addiction of any kind

These lists will seem obvious to many, but I have included them due to the number of great people I have known and whose career progression has been hindered by such issues.

****

Chapter 3: YOU versus the Unknown

In your life, you will be facing a number of obstacles: some will be physical, such as fighting a cold to attend an important meeting; others will be mental, such as figuring out the hidden traps in a contract; and yet others will be random and unpredictable, such as getting the right opportunity at the right time. This chapter focuses on the third point: YOU dealing with the unknown.

Let's travel back in time to May 1998 and consider Anne, a typical Columbia Business School MBA graduate. Anne has many job offers, all attractive, in various fields, and she can choose what she wants to do in life: we are in the middle of the internet boom, venture capital is flourishing, management consulting is in dire need of good human resources, investment banking is booming and there are all kinds of excellent offers at the great corporations of America. Anne is lucky to be entering the job market at the right time.

Using our time machine, let's go forward 11 years to May 2009 and consider Sophie, another typical Columbia Business School MBA Graduate. Sophie is as good as Anne, if not slightly better; except Sophie's choices (pardon the pun) are much more limited: Investment banking has been decimated by the financial crisis, most corporations are reeling from the recession, the venture capital field is in intensive care and management consulting now sees a lot more applicants for the same number of jobs. Sophie's problem is graduating at the wrong time.

Eventually, both Anne and Sophie will have great careers, but the fields in which they are, the money they make and the visibility they get will be influenced by opportunity and luck possibly as much as they are influenced by hard work and talent. As a talented and motivated individual, you will succeed no matter what; but the extent to which you will be able to use all your potential is heavily dependent on the chances you get.

While luck is random by definition, there are many ways to increase the probability that you will have it on your side:

- Being connected and visible makes more deals or opportunities go your way. Many job opportunities come from old acquaintances who have seen you on Facebook or Linked-In, many others from headhunters who have met you at an industry conference.
- Working in a growing field is more fertile in opportunities for you than working in a mature or stagnant industry.
- Being close to the decision-maker in your company gets you visibility in terms of any internal opportunities.

However, there is no way to positively guarantee luck and, no matter what you do, you will get bad breaks that have nothing to do with your performance:

- You could get passed over for a promotion because someone else comes from the same hometown as the CEO
- You could lose a job interview because you are perceived as overqualified and would therefore threaten the existing hierarchy
- You could get made redundant because your company had a huge loss in an area unrelated to you and has to cut everywhere.

If you've been working long enough, you know that all these things, and more, happen all the time.

Our focus now is not how to react to adversity; we will be dealing with that in another chapter. Our immediate concern is instead what mental attitude to adopt when so much of our future is at the hands of the unknown. We know we obviously cannot control the unknown, but we still need to function and we don't want the fear of the unknown to paralyze us!

I have devised an approach to deal effectively with the unknown; it is based on two orientations:

- A sense of duty
- A sense of fate

The sense of duty concept needs some explanation. If you look at why you would voluntarily do something, you will find that there are two major possible origins:

- A desire or wish
- A duty

You would eat a piece of chocolate, go see a nice movie, play some tennis or golf or read a good book because of desire or wish.

You would go into a boring meeting, visit your Alzheimer-afflicted grandaunt, listen to the policeman admonish you about speeding or help your daughter with her math homework because of duty.

There are many things that you do out of desire or duty at the same time: Eating is a duty and a pleasure, making love to your spouse is a duty according to many religions and it is usually also a pleasure! For the many of us who enjoy our work, performing it is a duty and a pleasure at the same time.

But why does it matter whether something is being done out of duty or out of desire? In order to answer that question, let's look at two characteristics of desire-based actions over duty-based actions:

- Choice: Doing something out of desire implies choice; you have a choice on whether you eat the ice cream or not. On the other hand, doing something out of duty implies there is no choice; it is your duty to feed your children, you don't have the choice of letting them go hungry.
- Guilt: Having a choice of doing or not doing something, and deriving pleasure out of doing it means you might feel guilty about it. By contrast, you cannot feel guilty for having done something that you are duty-bound to do and have no choice but to do! Even if doing it gives you pleasure!

It should by now be apparent that doing something out of duty is a lot less stressful than doing something out of desire: no choices to antagonize over, no guilt to contend with! But beyond reducing your stress levels, how do duty-based actions help with fear of the unknown?

To grasp this concept, imagine two people, each driving a car from a very remote place in Mexico to San Diego. These two people, John and Jack, have never met and will never meet. Both have been told that there is a remote possibility there might be bandits along the way who might take their car and their money and leave them stranded in the middle of nowhere. Both John and Jack have to reach San Diego urgently and have no choice but going with their car, so they both decide to make the trip anyway.

There is one big difference between John and Jack: John is told that there is only one way to reach San Diego and given a precise route that is easy to follow. Jack, on the other hand, is told that there are two different routes to San Diego and is given precise instructions that are easy to follow for each of the two routes. Jack is not given any information as to whether any of the two routes has a higher likelihood of meeting bandits than the other.

Now we all agree that both John and Jack will be stressed when on the journey. Which one will feel more stress: John who had no choice as to the route or Jack who selected his route between two possibilities? In my opinion, John, who had no options but to take this route will feel more relaxed than Jack, who will worry at every turn that he might have chosen the wrong route. In his book, "The Paradox of Choice: Why More is Less", writer Barry Schwartz makes a convincing case based on solid research that more options often lead to lower happiness.

Now if the bad outcome does happen and John and Jack both get attacked by bandits, how will each react to the situation?

- John will be upset and feel unlucky.
- Jack will also be upset and feel unlucky, but in addition will blame himself for having selected the wrong route,

even though he had no way of knowing to make a better selection!

So if you agree that more choice and more guilt increase stress levels, let's see how having a "sense of duty" is actually done and what it implies for you.

First, let me emphasize that I am only advocating this "sense of duty" orientation at work, not in your personal life, since my main observations of this concept have been work-related.

Second, let me emphasize that "sense of duty" is a state of mind: the only person you have to convince that your actions stem from duty is yourself, no one else.

So how does this work? Let's begin with an easy example that a large number of people still manage to screw up. Tina is in charge of trading at a small investment bank. She just discovered a major mistake in the trading positions of her team, which will probably cost the bank about 5 million dollars. What should she do?

- She might be tempted to hide the losses for a while to see if there is a way to recoup some of them.
- She might decide to tell her top management but wait until the right time to make the announcement.
- If she has the sense of duty we are looking for, she will recognize that her management needs to know immediately about the losses and will rush to inform them, knowing that she has no other choice.

That was an easy example, but the "sense of duty" concept can be applied to many other more complex situations. I think I first adopted this concept when I worked at Booz.Allen & Hamilton (now Booz & Co.). In retrospect, I believe it to be an unrecognized portion of the Booz culture. Let me make this point more explicit:

Booz consultants, as I suspect all top tier management consultants, have to work on assignments for other companies

38

such as: how can we reduce our cost structure and yet improve service levels, or why do we have such a high turnover in human resources and how could we reduce that turnover without raising compensation or possibly how can we enter the Chinese market and make profits? Booz's fees are very high, so individual consultants are billed to the client for up to 15 times what the client pays its own employees! This means that Booz consultants are usually subjected to three major stress sources:

(1) The stress of dealing with a new assignment with no guarantee that you will find the root of the problem you are analyzing and therefore be able to make the value-adding recommendations your client is looking for. For example, what if you are unable to find out why so many of your client employees want to leave?

(2) The stress of presenting your recommendations, some of which could be unpopular with your client. For example, what if you found out that the reason so many employees are unhappy is because the CEO - who hired you – has put in place, against the advice of his direct report, a very implausible incentive scheme? You want to recommend scrapping that scheme, but you obviously worry about his reaction!

(3) The stress of proving your value: you are billed 15 times more than the company executive who works with you, provides the data for you and participates in the recommendation. Because you are temporary and he is permanent, and because of your Booz training, anybody would understand your costing 5 times more. That leaves 3 times unexplained, which coincides with the fact that Booz is paying you about 3 times what the client is paying him. Are you 3 times smarter? Do you work 3 times more?

The answer to these stress sources is the sense of duty I have observed at Booz and later adopted in my professional life:

(1) In dealing with the stress of being able to find the problem and resolve it, Booz consultants tend to adopt a fatalistic, "sense of duty" attitude: we need to deploy a competent team, organize ourselves, formulate our hypotheses and look at all the data conscientiously, work efficiently and hard, ask the right questions and we are confident that we will get the insights that will deliver

value to the client. We have done thousands of assignments and we have almost never been unable to find those insights. It's a little bit like the army: we do our duty, and, God willing, we will win the battle.

(2) In dealing with the stress of presenting the correct recommendation, the "sense of duty" is even more apparent: we are paid to present the truth, not what the client wants to hear. It is our duty to tell the client what we believe and up to him to accept, or not, our recommendations. Sugar coating, of course, may be an option, but making a different recommendation is not an option.

(3) In dealing with the stress of proving their value, consultants also, unconsciously, adopt a "sense of duty" attitude: the vast majority of them either work very long hours or work normal hours very intensely and very efficiently. You will rarely find Booz consultants making small talk at the water-cooler, unless such small talk is necessary for the assignment.

In my every day life, sense of duty means:

- No "scratch my back and I'll scratch yours" deals with any colleague
- My opinion on a subject doesn't vary according to my audience
- If my institution has a problem that I am most qualified to resolve, I will attempt to resolve it as best I can. I will not shy away from problems because they are too politically risky or because they have a high probability of failure. In a country at war, the best generals should be at the front, not working on some side project because it is safer.

****

Avoidance: The "Wishful Thinker" Syndrome

Gerard, a star analyst in London, is voicing his amazement: "I follow about 15 companies and get invited to their investors' conferences. About 7 are both honest and objective about their upcoming results, meaning they can predict the nest quarter's earnings within a small margin of error. 5 others predict rosy earnings, but it is apparent that their figures are embellished for our benefits and that they really are expecting lower numbers. It is the remaining 3 that amaze me: their CEOs and CFOs offer numbers that any beginner in the industry would know to be exaggerated, and yet they seem to believe them! It is as if the entire management of those companies was on some kind of drugs! And when their actual numbers do come out way lower than expectations, they blame it on some fluke and continue business as usual,…until somebody at the board level pushes the eject button, and the CEO or someone else in management gets fired!"

A similar story from Sharon, a real estate broker: "I have a type of customer that I call Willy. Willy will invariably look for a home way above his budget. When I try to convince him that he would have trouble getting a mortgage for this property, he invariably disagrees; when I then tell him that even if he did get the mortgage, he would have trouble making the payment, he tells me not to worry. He seems to think that some kind of income will be materializing for him at some point in the immediate future, though he can't pinpoint any source for that hypothetical income. After 20 years in the business, when I do meet a Willy, I channel him to another broker!"

A final story from Claude, a high-school advisor: "So many students are what I call wishful thinkers: a mere two weeks before their finals, they come up with very rosy predictions for their final grades. I explain to them that even if they study 24/7, there is no way for them of making these grades given their performance so far during the year. They usually look at me as if I was speaking a foreign language and go away. When they don't get their predicted grades, they get so surprised!"

The common thread in the three stories above: wishful thinkers. We have all been guilty of wishful thinking at some point or another during our lives. In fact, I deliberately use wishful thinking to avoid wasting energy on a problem I consider trivial or nonessential. This type of avoidance is very productive and allows you to focus on core issues, as the next chapter will show you. The problem is that we sometimes use wishful thinking to avoid dealing with major issues that can be detrimental to our core activities.

Of course, as a number of studies have shown, being optimistic is a strength and being negative is usually self-fulfilling in that negative people tend to be mediocre. However, positivism should be accompanied by a high degree of energy and resolve, whereas wishful thinking smacks of laziness.

Life is structured in three dimensions: positive, negative and neutral; like, dislike and indifference; up, down and flat. In terms of work or relationships, these three dimensions are: action, escape and avoidance. All three are necessary in specific circumstances and avoidance can help you focus provided the issues you choose to avoid are not core issues.

For more on being positive and effective, read on…

****

Chapter Four: Focusing YOU

Up to 5% of our children are afflicted with ADHD (Attention Deficit Hyperactivity Disorder). This disorder makes them impulsive, unfocused, overactive and affects their classroom performance as well as their relationships with friends and parents. Fortunately, the problem can be treated (and is not the focus of this book). While ADHD in children and in some adults has been correctly identified and dealt with by members of the educational community, I see milder forms of ADHD in executives and business people that are going totally unnoticed.

One of the CEOs I have worked with has a total inability to focus: Albert, as we will call him, is a perfectionist. Because of this characteristic, and his forcefulness, his board of directors used to admire him. Unfortunately, his direct reports quickly discovered that he was impossible to work with. Take his Chief Information Officer as an example: He approached Albert with a to-do-list of IT initiatives and explained to him that he did not have enough resources to tackle all the initiatives on the list in a reasonable timeframe. He was expecting Albert to prioritize items for him, tell him for example to start with closing security loopholes that endangered the company and leave fixing the layout on the HR application for later. Instead, Albert dismissed the CIO and told him that if he was incapable of doing his job he would replace him. Same with the Planning Manager, who was asked to launch a huge number of products in a tiny timeframe and with the Chief Financial Officer who had to juggle with more projects than budgets could handle. Albert's "I want everything" approach cost him a huge turnover in management ranks resulting in business slowdown and operational errors and eventually cost him his job.

Some of you may have seen an auditor's report (or a risk manager's report) concerning a company or a business unit and may have found it so complete with accurate observations that you may have wondered why the auditor or the risk manager was not himself the unit or company CEO: after all, if he was so good at identifying weaknesses, he would probably be excellent at fixing them. In my experience, the problem with many of these auditor-types (or consultant-types) is that they are so scared of having anyone point out a shortcoming to them that they become incapable of choosing a priority to the detriment of another.

It is, however, a reality that we live in a world of scarce resources and limited time and that a key success factor for us as individuals is how we allocate our time and resources among competing projects, i.e. how we focus.

A great illustration of focus is Booz&Co's hypothesis-driven approach. When I joined Booz, I imagined assignments to go through the following cycle:

1. Client has a problem and requests Booz's assistance in resolving it

2. Booz collects data, analyzes it and identifies the problem

3. Booz presents findings and recommendations

Actually, assignments go through a slightly different cycle:

1. Client has a problem and requests Booz's assistance in resolving it

2. The Booz&Co team, with some client counterparts, conducts a brainstorming session and outlines hypotheses on what the client problem might be

3. Booz collects data that would either confirm or infirm the outlined hypotheses

4. Based on the data, Booz confirms the problem

5. Booz presents findings and recommendations

In my first few days on the job, I had difficulty grasping the hypothesis concept. I would ask other employees: "Why not just collect data with an open mind? What if the real problem is very different from our hypotheses? Why begin an assignment with preconceived ideas?" The response was invariably: "We do not have time to go on fishing expeditions. Between all of us as a team, there is sufficient experience that our hypotheses will come out very close to the solution, and that will make the data gathering that much more efficient. Besides, even if our hypotheses are wrong, the data will tell us in what direction to push." After dozens of assignments, I can testify that this approach always yielded results and saved assignments from becoming aimless wanders.

When you are trying to bend a spoon, you have to focus your energy on

44

two points to exercise pressure on one area of the spoon. Because of the focus of all your strength on one spot, you are able to bend the spoon. Famous performer Uri Geller used to appear in shows and bend spoons and keys using only his mental concentration. Subsequent skeptics have later accused him of using magic tricks to perform his feats, but the mere fact that many of you are prepared to believe it could be done is an indication of what one can do using concentration and focus.

In his book, "Trading in the Zone: Maximizing Performance with Discipline and Focus", psychiatrist and top trading coach Ari Kiev, argues that traders can create a state of mind that will improve their performance. My friend Waleed, who is a backgammon champion, shares Dr. Kiev's beliefs and goes one step further: "When I am really focused on my game, I feel that I can even influence the dice. So if I need a 6-3, I'll throw the dice and get a 6-3. I often know what my opponent's dice will show before they stop rolling!"

If you watch Rhonda Byrne's movie, "The Secret", you'll see a number of people testifying to great accomplishments they were able to make by believing in themselves and focusing on what they wanted to accomplish. In one example, someone focused on receiving money and received an unexpected check in the mail a few days later. As I was watching the movie, I remembered thinking "How could this happen to me now, since I am aware of all my sources of income and none of them includes checks that could be mailed?" Ironically, 2 or 3 weeks later, I did receive a check in the mail: I had made a mistake in my income tax return, and the government refunded me an additional amount of more than a thousand dollars!

Outside of this incident, I do have the feeling, in my daily work, that if I focus enough on a problem, I can make it unravel.

Of course, focusing on a problem to make it go away entails approaching the problem with a positive attitude and believing in your power to resolve it. Obsessing about a problem can have the opposite effect, as the movie "The Secret" will tell you and as I have found out for myself observing my close friend Mildred. The following true story will be as revealing for you, I hope, as it was for me: At the time of the story, Mildred was a beautiful woman of 45 who looked 35. Mildred had an ideal weight that never fluctuated, according to the scale in her bathroom that she uses on a daily basis. Invariably, the number is always the same and most people who see Mildred daily agree that she always looks the same. For some reason, however, Mildred began obsessing about her weight, believing that she was losing too much weight and looking too skinny. While her real weight never fluctuated, it so happened that Mildred went through a phase in which she received, on an approximately weekly basis, comments from people who barely knew her, such as "Oh my God, why have you lost so much weight?" She would tell me about these incidents regularly, sometimes describing how she answered back with responses such as "What business is it of yours how much I weigh?" or "I barely know you, how can you make such comments?" I would pause and think:

- My own weight fluctuates much more than Mildred's (which, I repeat, doesn't fluctuate at all)

- Yet very few people ever comment about my weight to me, and most of those are really close friends or family.

- How is it, then, that Mildred is able to get all those perfect strangers to comment to her about her weight?

There can be, in my opinion, only two possibilities: either Mildred is a pathological liar and all these comments never happened, or Mildred's obsession is telepathically influencing people who are not close to her. Since I know Mildred is not a liar, there is only one explanation left for me!

In order to focus, you need to prioritize. In order to prioritize, you have to let yourself downgrade any of your goals that are not crucial. In my various stints as CEO and business unit head, I have found it most effective to focus on 2-3 great initiatives while keeping everything else in maintenance mode. This singularity of purpose has always achieved great results for me. Sometimes I even feel that looking hard enough at a problem can resolve it.

Focus also means zooming in quickly on any problems that develop. No business offers a trouble-free environment in which you can work on your own priorities at your own leisure; every now and then, you are bound to encounter a crisis or series of issues that will distract you from your immediate goals. Ignoring these problems makes them grow bigger, so the simplest solution is to tackle them immediately. I am amazed at the number of otherwise successful people who are able to totally ignore such problems, and let them linger to the point where they become too big to solve.

46

Identifying a major problem, then focusing on its resolution is a great way to yield quick results. My daughter went from a C+ to an A student in middle-school math by changing the way she studied:

- Initially, she would first review the items she understood, do their related exercises, and then start looking at items she had not grasped very well. That's when she was a C+ student.

- She later changed her mode of operation: she started focusing first on items she had not fully understood and would review other concepts only after the first set was fully within her grasp. Her grades immediately jumped to A.

Unfortunately, many people try to escape their real issues by giving their attention to "fake problems" which are easy to resolve and give the impression of accomplishment. Some examples:

- The head of a sales team who spends more time on the design of forms than on identifying and contacting sales targets. The need for a perfect sales support infrastructure is a great escape candidate for sales management staff who are afraid of going against challenging targets.

- The head of operations for a major financial service firm who has real customer service problems but is waiting for IT to fix the software before cleaning all the problems. Looking for a scapegoat elsewhere in the organization is another favorite excuse to procrastinate.

- The CEO of a corporation who spends most of his time in large meetings involving all the key executives of the company. Meetings are a great way to spread responsibilities and appear busy even as nothing gets done; some executives are so addicted to meetings that a new word, "meetingitis" has been coined to describe the propensity of dysfunctional organizations to conduct unnecessary meetings!

As I mentioned earlier, auditors are often poster boys for lack of focus: Recently, I found out a glaring security gap in the IT infrastructure of a company I was involved with. The gap was so evident that it defied common sense: 20 people had been given the system user ID and password which meant that any of these people could access the system's database and no one could know who did! Worse, even employees who had left the company had the ID and password since no one had bothered to change it. I called the company's chief auditor to see what were his comments since he had recently audited IT and, to my surprise, found that he had correctly identified the problem. Unfortunately, he had buried his findings under 20 pages of other findings, many of which were trivial!

Identifying priorities is a key success factor in being focused. Some procrastinators will tell you they are focused, but you will discover that their priorities are different from yours. In identifying priorities, it helps to classify issues by level:

- Level 1 priorities, the most crucial, are items that are causing you to lose money or have a large probability to cause you to lose money. For example, if you have a major scandal involving the company or a business unit losing money in a big way or a fire in the building, that's a level 1 priority, one you should attend to before anything else!

- Level 2 priorities are the major drivers for your company to go forward. What are the 2 to 3 key success factors that will make your company successful? What businesses are crucial to the company future? What competitive advantage should be developed or improved? Of course, level 2 priorities can be defined according to your function within the company; for example, if you were in sales, they would be your key accounts or your key prospects. If you were in audit, they would be the 2-3 key threats in each area you are reviewing.

- Level 3 priorities are important issues that are neither level 1 nor level 2, but might one day grow to reach a critical level. You should deploy resources against level 3 priorities but give them your attention only after you've attended to the other 2.

Keeping these priority levels separate and distinct in your mind and your communications will greatly enhance your focus and therefore your performance. It will also ensure that you and your team can "see the forest for the trees" and communicate that vision company wide.

In his book, "Embracing the Sky", autistic genius and author Daniel Tammet, attributes both the handicaps of autists and their incredible exploits involving math and languages to their attraction to the smallest details: "I see the scratches on a table's surface before seeing the entire table; the reflection of a light on a window before I perceive the whole window; the patterns on a carpet before the whole carpet comes into view." Achieving successful focus means looking at the big picture first and then zooming in, not the opposite!

A quick test of how focused you are is your response to this question: "There are good news and bad news, which do you want to hear first?" If you usually answer "bad news", you are probably focused because bad news could come from "level 1" issues and you should tackle them first, whereas "good news" probably relate to "level 2" at best. If you usually answer "good news", you may have an escape or avoidance problem where you have difficulty facing reality.

Hearing the news is not enough: how quickly you react to bad news is also a sign of your effectiveness as a person. In my early days in Private Banking, I was sharing an office with a colleague who was told to advise his biggest client that some of his funds under management had incurred a loss due to unforeseen market reversals. I was waiting for my colleague, Bob, to make that important phone call, as I was keen on seeing how he would handle it, having been in similar situations myself. I had to wait a long time as Bob was in no hurry to make that call. After a few hours of watching Bob procrastinate, I lost my nerves and yelled at him to make the call! He was bewildered by my behavior since I was not his supervisor but after a brief altercation with me, finally summoned up enough courage to make the call.

In my experience, Bob is a very typical executive: There are more procrastinators than doers in the business world.

There are many other indicators of focus:

- Being on time to appointments is a sign that you have your priorities straight and are in control of your environment.

- Being able to explain what you need in a short memo or orally in just a few phrases is a sign that you know what you want and have your act together.

- Being able to make decisions quickly without the need to revisit them is also a sign that you know where you're going. While it is important to be flexible, constant reassessment of past decisions can be very counterproductive.

If you are unfocused, then focusing will greatly improve your effectiveness. If you've decided to focus, it is of course crucial that you focus on the right issues. Key to that is proper planning.

Back in the late 1990s, I was watching a tennis match on TV. One of the two players was a young Russian. I unfortunately forgot his name but he was in the world top ten rankings at that period of time. He was playing against a strong opponent, but my interest in the match came from watching him: he was not very well built, didn't look very athletic, was not a great server or net player and had no particular shot that would explain his great performance; yet, he was beating some outstanding players and I wanted to know why. After a few minutes of watching, I was able to understand why: he had an uncanny ability to know where the ball was going, so he would move to that spot very early and be ready to return the ball very quickly. His key strength was his anticipation.

In the business world, proper anticipation is a key asset. Much like the trial lawyer who is taught never to ask a question unless she knew the answer, you should usually try to predict the reaction of others before you have a conversation with them. This is not impossible to do, it just takes some practice. For me, Booz's hypothesis driven approach was great practice: even client meetings were planned and client reactions were anticipated. In fact, a client presentation was usually called a failure if the client gave any comment the Booz team didn't anticipate or already know.

I once made a great impression on my deputy, Jocelyne. Jocelyne had just stepped into her role as deputy head of retail banking and was planning to ask Tony, our very talented Chief Information Officer whose solutions have dramatically raised our competitiveness, to consider automating a credit card process that we had been doing manually. I was rushing into a meeting, so I told her the following: "He's going to ask you how many transactions are affected by the process, so be sure to take the statistics with you. Then, he's going to ask you how fast you need it, so you'll tell him you need it quickly. At that point, he'll ask you if you are willing to postpone the automation of the car loan document processing to speed up this one and you'll say you absolutely need the car loan process as urgently. He'll then need to think about it, so try to fix another appointment with him for the second discussion."

On my return from my meeting, I found a hilarious Jocelyne waiting for me.

- "What's so funny?"

50

- "How did you do it?!"

- "How did I do what?"

- "How did you know what he was going to say?"

- "Who?"

- "Tony! He responded exactly as you told me, so I was trying to contain my laughter the whole time. The meeting followed the exact script you anticipated!"

The three or four minutes of thinking required to anticipate what is likely to happen in a meeting or an event can save you countless hours of additional meetings and data preparation. Besides, becoming good at anticipating and predicting will improve your strategic focus: your hunches and intuition will become more accurate.

To grasp the concept of focus, it is helpful to think of a road. Imagine if somebody tells you: Just walk this road until you reach its end, and all your dreams will come true. That would be great! School was a little bit like that: all you had to do was study hard and success was at the end of the school year. The business world is, unfortunately, much more complex: you could be working very hard but be in the wrong industry, the wrong market or the wrong product... and fail. So when you do find yourself in business situation where you have identified the right issues, consider it a blessing... and focus!

In the business world, there will be initiatives that succeed no matter what, because they happen to take place in the right market at the right time. There will be other initiatives that fail no matter what, because they are too early or in the wrong market. My experience, however, is that most initiatives will succeed or fail because of the effort and focus you invest behind them. If you focus enough, it is unlikely that you will have many failures.

A final word about focus: your environment will be constantly trying to pry you away from your focus, because other people have different priorities and agendas. Being focused doesn't mean being stubborn or inflexible. You will often question yourself and feel lonely, and maybe that's where the saying "It's lonely at the top" comes from. But, if you know you're going in the right direction, you have to keep the faith, and the focus!

****

Escape: Getting the Correct Dosage

Timmy is a highly dedicated investment banker. He works very long hours and has practically no time for any social life. His one major escape is movies or the theatre, where he goes about twice a week. When he is watching a movie or a play, he is so concentrated that he feels like having left his body and joined the cast of characters on the scene. For about two hours, he lives the life of somebody else. Then he goes home and sleeps, and he dreams of the movie or play, and wakes up the next day all fresh and ready to work.

This is Timmy's main escape, enabling him to cope with the stress of a high pressure job. There are other forms of escape, such as a vacation, a seminar, a sports game, exercise, etc. You will probably readily agree with me on the following:

- Some form of escape is essential to remain creative and productive.

- Too much escape is harmful: taking a two-week vacation every year is useful, being on vacation for six months every year is destructive.

Moving on to more controversial grounds, let's call the above forms of escape "conscious escape", as opposed to "subconscious escape".

Subconscious escape is an activity or emotion that effectively detracts from your main conscious path, but appears to you to have some other legitimate goal. Examples of subconscious escape: unnecessary meetings, frivolous disputes, obsession with a trivial matter, mid-life crisis, addictions of any kind, too much interest in office gossip, etc.

What could make you have subconscious escapes?

- Possibly, you are not getting enough conscious escapes, you are overworked, you are getting bored.

- Or you do not like your job, you unconsciously want to fail.

In any case, you should make an effort to objectively identify your subconscious escapes and quantify their impact on your overall productivity.

If the impact is small, keep doing what you're doing: remember, escape in small quantities is beneficial.

If the impact is large, you should assess the cause: plan for more time off and more outside interests in order to move your escape needs from the realm of the subconscious to the conscious.

If that doesn't help, review chapter one, Aligning YOU, and work on your alignment problems.

****

Chapter 5: Transactions and Emotions

My father suddenly fell on the ground during a family gathering. *My mother, my sister, my brother and I were all very shaken.* We laid him on the ground while we called an ambulance. *We were very worried as we waited for the ambulance to arrive.* The ambulance arrived and took him to the hospital. *We were relieved that he was able to breathe and talk, despite feeling dizzy.* The doctor saw him and declared that he was in his last stage (he had advanced Parkinson's and was 88). *We felt sad and resigned.* I sat down with him to say my goodbyes, and he gave me his last wishes. *I felt down but still lucky to have had the chance to properly say goodbye.* Later, he deceased. *Again, I felt sad but serene.* We went through a week of burial and condolences at home and at Church. *I was touched by the presence of all our friends and family...*

My friend Alexis met Anne-Marie at his best friend Jim's house (she was Jim's girlfriend's sister). *He immediately felt a strong attraction for her.* He began to talk to her and express his emotions (Alexis is very straightforward). *She was initially rebuked by the attention as it was too sudden* and therefore did not reciprocate the attention. *Not easily discouraged, Alexis felt even more pumped up.* He remained at her side, cracking jokes and generally being cute. *She was flattered by the attention.* They went out several times after that. *Both were feeling in love.* Finally, Alexis popped the question. *Anne-Marie thought she was going to faint.* She accepted. *Alexis felt on top of the world.* They prepared a great wedding together and received all the friends and family. *In addition to being elated about being married, they were very touched by the participation and encouragement of friends and family...*

What do these two paragraphs have in common and why all these italics? They are an illustration of what seems to be a law of nature: All transactions give rise to emotions and all emotions in turn are followed by transactions. I have italicized the emotions in each paragraph to illustrate the alternation between emotions and transactions.

It seems evident that all transactions give rise to emotions: we are saddened by tragic events; we are uplifted by positive events. Can you think of any material event that doesn't give rise to an emotion? Since I can't, I won't belabor the subject, so let's agree with the first law: All transactions give rise to emotions.

Less obvious is the second law: All emotions are followed by transactions. So, let's give a few examples to illustrate:

- Your child is sick. He comes to you crying and you feel bad. Your heart is torn apart and you wish you were sick in his place. You know that there isn't much to do as this is an ordinary cold, but you feel the obligation to do something, so you either take him to a doctor or you buy him a toy or you bake him his favorite cake. The point is, you have to DO SOMETHING.

- We've often heard these two words in times of extreme emotion: DO SOMETHING. It is extremely frustrating to be overcome by emotion and not be able to do anything.

- You get a nice promotion at work and you are ecstatic. Can you do nothing about it? No, you feel the need to go out and have a nice dinner, send roses to your husband or give yourself the luxury spa treatment you've been dreaming about. The point is, you have to DO SOMETHING.

So now if we have enriched our culture with two new laws, what do we do about them?

We'll begin with the first one: All transactions give rise to emotions.

If all transactions give rise to emotions, then all our actions translate into positive or negative emotions we are growing in other people. It would seem smart to multiply the positive emotions we hold with others while minimizing the negative emotions. Remember that positive emotions will later get back to us through transactions because of the second law while negative emotions will come back to haunt us in the same way.

So it would be stupid to act in a way that creates negative emotions in others while not bringing us any value. So making fun of a coworker for no reason, getting drunk and propositioning the receptionist, throwing things at subordinates on a regular basis are all stupid.

Likewise, if it doesn't cost you much to elicit positive emotions, you should do it every time. So if a presentation is good, be vocal about it. If you have tickets to a concert and you can't go, give them to someone who will. If the report you're looking at needs just a small tweak to become perfect and, for some reason, you're the only one who has noticed, tell the others without making a big deal out of it.

More interesting is what we can do with the second law: All emotions are followed by transactions.

This law has implications for how you react. In my early days, it was very fashionable to talk about restraining your emotions; acting corporate meant suppressing feelings and remaining subdued. Gurus would teach you to control your emotions and books carried such titles as "The Unemotional Investor".

However, if emotions are a source of energy, it makes sense to me that you should USE YOUR EMOTIONS.

If you have made the effort to go through an alignment exercise with your subconscious mind, and are therefore confident that your subconscious mind is not following a different agenda, then your emotions are in turn aligned with your conscious agenda. If so, it makes sense for you to trust these emotions and let them propel your actions.

An athlete who is playing in front of his home crowd and is being cheered enthusiastically will be experiencing a rush of emotion. Fighting the emotion is not only unproductive, it is counterproductive: in order to fight an energy flow, you have to use energy, and that weakens you. By contrast, if you use that energy flow, it makes you stronger. That is why there is such a thing as a home court advantage.

Let's go through a concrete example of using your emotions: You are an advertising executive and your team has lost a major account, not because your performance was substandard but because of a special relationship your competitor has with one of your customer's influential board members. You and your team are fuming and angry. You could:

- Get out to a nearby bar and get completely plastered, then get into a fight with some other people at the bar and come back home at 3 AM completely wasted and exhausted and unable to work for the next two days.

OR

56

- Get your team into a meeting room and give yourselves a month to replace that account with at least two other accounts, then make a plan and assign responsibilities with the actual process of achieving the goals starting immediately.

If you opt for the first solution, you have not only wasted your emotion, you have used it in a self-destructive manner. That's what losers do.

If you opt for the second solution, there is a big chance that you will find yourself in a month or two in a better situation than before the loss of the account. That's how winners win.

The next chapter will delve deeper into the topic of rebounding from losses; in this one, we are more concerned about using our emotions. Let us look at another example, this time involving positive emotions: You have just received a big promotion and been identified as a key executive at your company. You are overjoyed and ecstatic. You could:

- Invite your spouse and your common friends to a Champagne dinner at the most expensive restaurant in your town. After the dinner, make mad love to your spouse and begin planning a great vacation together. The next day, book the vacation for immediately afterwards. Show up next to work two weeks later.

OR

- Buy a great gift for your spouse and take him/her to a romantic dinner, followed by mad lovemaking. In the next few days, schedule a series of lunches and dinners with (a) the people who were instrumental in your work success to thank them for what they have done for you and find out what they expect from you going forward and (b) the people you will be working with after your promotion to understand them and see how you can be successful in your next role.

If you opt for the first solution, you have rewarded yourself and your spouse, both of which are very important for your long-term equilibrium, but have not gained anything else.

If you opt for the second solution, you have also rewarded yourself and your spouse; but you have developed, in addition, valuable goodwill (positive emotions) with your current and future colleagues and more insight on how to meet expectations in the future. You have a heads up on your next role.

Using your emotions does not mean rushing your decisions! Decisions should only be made after being extremely carefully prepared, much like an army should not initiate a war unless it has fully anticipated enemy reaction, preparedness levels and possible casualties. So don't use your emotions as an excuse to make rash decisions; rather, use them to increase the speed of your preparation in anticipation of a decision.

So far, we have assumed that the intensity of the emotions is independent of us. For example, when my father died, I felt some emotions the intensity of which I cannot control.

Actually, I would argue that we control, at least through our subconscious mind, the intensity of our emotions. A good example of that is a friend of mine, Robert, who plays chess, among his many other hobbies. One day Robert surprised me by attracting my attention to the fact that when he is playing a game of chess, against someone of comparable level, his pulse runs at about 110 beats per minute, which is the equivalent level for him of his heartbeat immediately after running 400 meters! This is because the intensity of concentration that he needs when playing chess requires a strong emotional energy.

Apparently, when we know we have something to accomplish that requires major energy, we work up the emotion beforehand. For example, if you need to announce to your boss that there is a major mistake in the presentation he has just given, you feel a huge emotion prior to the event. This emotion is what pushes you and gives you the courage to make the revelation to your boss knowing that, whatever his reaction, you will feel a huge sense of relief for having told him!

So if we can control the intensity of our emotions, it makes sense to try to use emotions sparingly; be efficient with our emotions! To understand the point, let's establish a parallel between oil and emotions.

In the past, oil was viewed as a useless, stinky, dirty, toxic substance that one should avoid. Likewise, emotions were viewed as a hindrance to objectivity and to unbiased decision-making and therefore should be eliminated from the workplace.

Then came the realization that oil is a major source of energy and humanity started using oil to power vehicles, generate electricity, develop chemicals, etc. It became hard to imagine the world without oil! Likewise, emotions are a source of energy that should be harnessed and utilized by us if we want to maximize our output at the personal or professional levels!

However, oil is scarce and emits pollution; so using it as a source of energy is no excuse for using it inefficiently: we should create cars that are energy-efficient, use alternative sources of energy if they are cheaper and less polluting, etc. Likewise, emotions are not a cost-free source of energy: negative emotions can be stressful, causing tension and lack of sleep. For your physical and mental health, and for the sanity of your work environment, you should strive to be emotion-efficient, meaning that a little emotion can take you a long way.

I have met a number of people who are so emotion-inefficient as to become dysfunctional. One of them, Christine, gets so emotional before doing the tiniest task that she is completely wasted at the end of the working day. In addition, she is totally unable to perform stressful tasks because the emotion she would require is unsafe for her and for her environment. I suspect Christine has some unresolved issues with her subconscious mind.

Emotion efficiency is a goal you have to work on to achieve: through training, self-persuasion, introspection and even physical fitness.

With time and experience, you should become more emotion-efficient, and be able to do your work with an increasingly lower level of emotions. I recently made the decision to demote an employee who had not been performing up to standard. My mind was at ease with the decision: I had given the guy many chances, his performance was causing a problem for others in his unit and the decision meant that someone else would be given a chance to run the unit. However, it is always difficult to tell someone he would be demoted. On the day I announced my decision to him, I was surprised at how quiet the session went: I announced the

59

event very matter-of-factly, stressing that the decision was without recourse, but explaining the reasons that had driven me to make such a decision. In turn, he reacted very calmly and thanked me for the fact that I had decided to keep him in the division despite the bad performance. The emotional level on my side was relatively low given the circumstances and on his side relatively low as well given the finality of the decision. If I had been more emotional, he would have been more emotional as well, possibly yelling or crying and it would have spoiled the better part of the day for both of us.

This example is a good illustration of the final point to make about emotions, which is that they seem to be contagious: If you yell at someone, he will probably yell back. If you're in a playful, happy mood, people with you will probably smile and joke.

You have probably met Norman, there is at least one of him in every office: Norman is always complaining and generally depressed: for Norman, the system can't do anything right and the management is a closed club, dead set against him and the likes of him. Because Norman never changes his speech, he spreads discouragement wherever he goes.

You don't want to be like Norman and you don't want to be around Norman. If Norman is on your team, talk to him about changing his behavior. You should be, especially if you're a manager, the opposite of Norman: be the first to set the mood in any environment by being in a good mood, by being positive, by offering compliments to people around you. The positive energy you spread will translate into higher loyalty, higher productivity and a longer, healthier life for people around you.

****

The Emotion Waster

You have probably met more than one Bernie in your life: Bernie is usually very pleasant, save for his annoying habit of recapping his latest major decisions and lamenting that he made the wrong decision.

Did Bernie buy a car recently? He will tell you that he has the wrong model because (a)his boss misled him about the car's specifications or (b)his wife insisted on that particular model, even though it is technically inferior.

Did his wife change the color of the living room? He doesn't like the new color, but doesn't hate it so much that she should switch back to the old one.

At work, Bernie will wait until a report is submitted and then begin to lament its inaccuracies and grammatical errors. If his colleagues launch a new product, he will be quick to pinpoint to them his negative views on it, after the launch is completed.

Not surprisingly, he is often the victim of unpleasant remarks from his wife or his coworkers.

If you point out to him that he is counterproductive given that his feedback is too late for anyone to do anything about it, he answers by extolling the virtues of self-criticism. You end up avoiding him, which saves you time and energy.

****

Chapter 6: Capitalizing on Adversity

It strikes me that there are usually three phases of evolution that we can observe in our known history.

In the first phase, man discovers adversity and is beaten by it: Many of our early ancestors have died of cold, of sunstrokes, of drowning, etc.

In the second phase, man begins to find ways to beat adversity: clothing to protect from the cold, hats to protect from sunstrokes, boats to cross the seas, etc. We have become very refined in beating adversity with the use of air conditioners, quake-resistant buildings, noise insulation, etc.

We are currently entering the third phase, in which we are not so focused on beating adversity as much as we are focused on using adversity: windmills to generate energy, solar panels to provide heat, trash and waste being recycled to provide fertilizer and energy. The movement of waves is currently being used to provide energy. I believe that, in the future, extreme cold and extreme heat will also be sources of energy as will noise, pollution, the greenhouse effect and virtually every major source of annoyance.

Medicine is still in the second phase: we are living longer and healthier thanks to great wins over many diseases and we are making new strides in fighting disease every day, but, based on what I see happening in other sciences, I believe a third phase is coming when we will be using viruses and cancer as sources of energy!

Which brings us to life, business and relationships. In all these fields, we are currently using adversity as a source of energy! Examples of that abound, as will be clear from the many I am providing below:

One of Eric Clapton's greatest songs, and certainly my favorite, "Tears in heaven", was written after his young son, Conor, who was only four years old, fell to his death from the 53rd floor of a Manhattan skyscraper in 1991. That year, Clapton received 6 Grammy awards for that song and a related album. Clearly, not even writing the world's most beautiful song can compensate you for the loss of a child, but there is no denying that Clapton's overwhelming grief did produce a masterpiece.

The ultimate in adversity, death, yours or that of a significant loved one will obviously devastate you. Short of that, however, adversity can be good for you. I am a strong believer in the saying: "What doesn't kill you makes you stronger!" The saying actually comes from German philosopher Friedrich Nietzsche's original quote: "What doesn't destroy me makes me stronger"; and Nietzsche should know since his life was full of ups and downs, including major illnesses and rejections from publishers and readers. On this front, Asian culture and wisdom have an edge over their Western counterparts: Many centuries before Nietzsche, the Chinese recognized the energy potential of adversity. The word "crisis" is written in Chinese using two ideograms: The top one is the ideogram used for "danger" and the bottom one is the ideogram for "opportunity". In other words, crisis is composed of both danger and opportunity. This means that, if you are able to survive danger, crisis brings you opportunity.

In 1985, Michael Milken was on top of the world: As the inventor of a new financing instrument called junk bond, he had revolutionized the world of finance and engineered the Leveraged Buyout revolution that gave rise to the go-go eighties. He had propelled his employer, Drexel, to the top of the investment-banking world, and was earning bonuses of some 500 million dollars per year. He was one of the most powerful men in the world. However, he probably became too greedy and committed several securities law violations, so he ended up going to jail and Drexel collapsed. He was released from jail in January 1993 and was immediately afterwards diagnosed with prostate cancer, at the young age of 46. Interestingly, the diagnosis itself was a fluke: One of Milken's friends had just died of prostate cancer, so Milken asked his physician to perform a PSA test; the physician refused on the grounds that Milken was too young to be at risk, but Milken insisted. Unfortunately, the cancer had already spread to his lymph nodes, so his prognosis was that he had two years to live. Through hormone and radiation therapy, he was able to beat cancer and was still alive on November 29, 2004 when he was profiled in the Fortune article: "The Man who Changed Medicine". The article details Milken's efforts to fight prostate cancer through his foundation, the appropriately named Prostate Cancer Foundation (PCF). The foundation, which had raised $210 million through 2003 and had financed about 1100 projects, was at the time the world's largest sponsor of prostate cancer research. According to the article, "if the PCF were to own the projects it has been affiliated with over the past decade, the products that have resulted from research it has funded would make the foundation the third largest biotech company in the world."

Michael Milken is the perfect poster boy for this chapter. Let's recap his story with our comments:

He suffered a major adverse event that didn't kill him: Actually, he suffered two such events; he went to jail and had cancer. Let's concentrate on the cancer, which is the most adverse of the two and which appeared only days after he was released from jail. Imagine being finally out of prison and ready to live your life, and to learn that you have cancer and will die soon!

If he hadn't had this adverse event, the rest of his life would have been mediocre: As part of his sentence, he had been barred for life from working in the securities industry, so no chance for him to restart a career there. He would have been confined to investing his own money, perhaps succeeding in obtaining a good performance, but nothing to write home about. Fortune Magazine would probably never have written something meaningful about him and he would have been remembered in history as a greedy trader who launched a new investment vehicle.

The adverse event dramatically improved his life: The cancer so energized him that he created a foundation, raised a lot of money for it, and used it to dramatically improve cancer research. He impressed Fortune Magazine enough to be the subject of a feature article and will now be remembered forever as a man of good, responsible for saving thousands of lives. He was able to beat his innovation record in finance with an innovation record in medicine.

The Milken story is so powerful, it makes me ask myself: could this cancer have originated from Milken's subconscious mind? Something to think about…

Someone I strongly suspect is highly energized by adverse events is former president Bill Clinton. His start in life was not exactly stellar: his father, William Jefferson Blythe, Jr., died 3 months before Bill was born. His mother remarried a Roger Clinton who, according to Bill's autobiography "My Life", was a gambler and an alcoholic and abused

64

Bill's mother and half-brother Roger Jr. From there, Bill went on to become Governor of Arkansas at the young age of 32 and was then the youngest governor in the USA. On his way to winning the democratic primary, he was beset by rumors of an affair with Gennifer Flowers and was badly trailing the other candidates, but was still able to recover the lost ground and clinch the nomination, earning himself the nickname, "The comeback kid". His second term as president was marked by revelations of an affair with an intern named "Monica Lewinsky". The affair and his subsequent testimony about it were a major blow to his credibility and he was almost impeached. Despite this severe crisis, he was able to finish his term and had an approval rating of 66%, the highest end-of-office rating of any US president since World War II (as of this writing in 2010).

To recap: Adverse events are an energy source. They help motivate you and focus your strengths on a specific goal. You should use that energy to further your goals. That's not to say you should help these adverse events happen or cause them. Not at all: in fact, that would run counter to the sense of duty we discussed in a previous chapter. It is your duty to give your job and yourself the best possible care and to avoid these adverse events whenever you can. However, no one is immune from failure, sickness, accidents or adversity. Once they do happen, what I am advocating is to use the emotions they will engender to achieve something good. So I would advise Bill Clinton to avoid affairs that endanger his family and his credibility even if in his case he was able to survive the scandal. On the other hand, I do congratulate Bill Clinton on using the energy to focus on achieving great things in his presidency.

My own life has witnessed a number of adverse events I have used to improve myself:

- I was only 16 when the civil war began in Lebanon where I grew up. For the next 5 years, I had to survive a number of mortar attacks, including 2 shells that fell on my apartment building, a struggle to get electricity and water and a challenge to continue my school program and go to college. This is in addition to the daily trauma of living in a war zone, learning that a neighbor had been kidnapped and executed or that a close friend had fled the country, etc. The experience was probably crucial in building my drive to work hard, get accepted at Columbia, get an MBA and succeed in business.

- I was 21 and a student at Columbia when, one day, I woke up at 5 am with a severe chest pain, as if an elephant was sitting on my chest. Plus, my left arm was tinkling. The whole thing lasted for about 20 minutes and went away, only to come back that afternoon around 5 pm for another 20 minutes and the next morning at 5 am for 20 minutes. After that, I went to the infirmary where the physician diagnosed a pericarditis, an inflammation of the heart's envelope. Not to worry, he said, it's probably viral and will leave without a trace. Except he called me back the same day: some tests were consistent with pericarditis while others indicated a myocardial infarction, more commonly known as a heart attack! I was admitted to Saint Luke's Hospital the same day, and I spent a week there with one day being told I could play squash immediately, and the next being taken by wheelchair to my tests! I saw my dreams being quashed: Having a heart attack at 21 would probably mean a slow life and early death... Thankfully, the final diagnosis indicated viral pericarditis and the next few years confirmed it. I did spend 6 months recovering, having back pain and not completely believing I was out of the woods. The experience changed my whole life: I became very attuned to my body and especially my heart; I began to walk every day; I started working 8-10 hours a day instead of 10-12; I became kinder and more forgiving, more focused on achievement than on power. In short, the experience made me a better person.

So far, we have seen a number of examples of major adversity generating major improvement in its victim's life. However, you should note that even minor adverse events are energy generators that you can use to improve a situation. The work environment is a constant source of adverse events for you to capitalize on. I have recently made it a rule for me to use any setback not only to recover my losses, but also to get something more in the process. Some examples:

- When I was at Booz, I was often assigned on projects led by Ron Stride, the senior partner in charge of Asia. As most Booz partners, Ron believed in "pushing the envelope" in delivering the best possible value for the client. I am also a believer in delivering the best possible value for the client, but I have a poker face and always appear more relaxed than other consultants. While Ron enjoys my insights, my relaxed appearance usually encourages him to push me harder. On a particular assignment for a large Thai bank, we had a major divergence of opinion: I felt we were doing an outstanding job, and the client was appreciative; whereas Ron felt we could do better and push more state-of-the-art recommendations. We had a number of discussions that were very frustrating for me because he would not tell me what specific state-of-the-art material we could incorporate in the project, which is normal since I was the banking operations specialist and he was purposely and somewhat mischievously pushing me to do my best. He did, however, often mention the concept of more centralization, which was even more frustrating to me since I was not a great believer in centralization in this particular case. So, here I was, not getting credit for what I thought was an outstanding job I was doing, with the only way out being a path I was uncomfortable following! It was inconceivable for me to make a recommendation I didn't believe in, and to be fair, Ron would not have wanted me to compromise my principles, and so I was extremely frustrated. So frustrated that I would, for days at a time, dream up arguments on why centralization was not the wave of the future. In a Eureka moment, I wrote these arguments in the form of an article which I published in the "Journal of Retail Banking" in the Summer of 1994 under the heading "Revamping Centralized Processing". This prestigious publication enabled me to convince Ron, and had the added benefit of providing me with an aura of innovation with the client and within Booz & Co. The article is now part of my CV and credentials. Even today, there is a little Ron in me that is constantly asking whether I have sufficiently "pushed the envelope" on a particular task.

- In 2002, Lebanon's finances were deteriorating. BLOM Bank's chairman at the time became rightly concerned about retail lending, which was under my supervision. Since most of our loans were credit-insured, he began to scrutinize our credit insurance and detected certain loopholes, which in my mind were noncritical, but in his mind major. We had a major disagreement, but we weathered the crisis and reduced slightly our retail lending. The economic crisis ended in 2003 when a number of donor countries helped Lebanon and we resumed retail lending at full speed. I took advantage of the recovery and of our chairman's feelings to recommend disposing with credit insurance and taking the credit risk in-house, something that ended up both saving us a substantial sum of money and dramatically increasing service levels.

- Examples of smaller setbacks abound: a great subordinate for whom I couldn't obtain a good raise, a great product for which I couldn't secure enough promotional budget, a real estate developer who suddenly reneges on his agreement to sell us a great branch location, etc. In each case, I try to come out ahead of the original plan: a richer job with more exposure for the subordinate, a better product pitched at a more opportune time, a better location through another developer...

By now, it should be clear to you that adversity is a source of energy that you should exploit rather than fight. That doesn't mean that you should take big risks and invite adversity for the purpose of using its related adrenaline and energy. "In medio stat virtus" (Virtue is in the middle) is a

Latin proverb advocating being in the middle between two extremes. It has definite relevance when it comes to dealing with adversity. In the following paragraphs, I will describe three profiles to make this point clearer.

Sam likes to take chances: when he travels, he always leaves home at the last minute and usually catches the plane in extremis. Being in a predictable situation such as a barbecue with family and friends bores him to death, so he is always looking to go out with shady characters that have had some run-ins with the law. Financially, he is always on the edge, buying fancy cars and borrowing to go to nice escapades whenever he comes into some money. He enjoys dangerous sports and has had some fractures in his youth. At work, he delivers but his bosses complain that he is always demanding raises and talking to headhunters. He has changed jobs many times and has often endured periods of unemployment. With time, however, Sam is mellowing down, which is good news for the stress level of his family.

Rob is Sam's opposite: he doesn't like the unknown and does his best to control his environment. He has very defined routines, such as going out every Friday and sleeping late every Saturday. His set of friends is constant. At work, he plays it very safe and tries to get consensus and managerial approval before he commits to any step. He accepts adversity and controls his emotions, which means he rarely reacts in any significant manner. He has had a very stable career at the same employer since graduating from college. He is happy but often asks himself why some of his colleagues get promoted faster.

Roselle is a combination of both Rob and Sam. If she's going to the airport, she factors in any traffic jams or unforeseen accidents. She plays safe sports because she knows she can't afford to take time off for injuries or broken bones. She has a diversified group of friends and doesn't like routine. At work, she is not afraid to commit to a certain position or to take chances, but she chooses her battles carefully. She doesn't easily take no for an answer, but is a great listener. Setbacks seem to give her a new wind and she seems to always eventually come out on top. She has had more than one employer but has remained a fair amount of time at each and had a smooth career progression.

Sam thrives on adversity and courts it passionately. Adversity is his sole source of energy and has become an addiction. Sam is viewed by his peers, subordinates, bosses, suppliers and customers as unreliable. Rob, on the other hand, avoids adversity and shuns risk. Rob is viewed by his environment as reliable but uncharismatic and unlikely to dazzle. Together, Rob and Sam would form a good team, maybe even a dream team. Only Roselle, with her sense of balance and healthy respect yet fearlessness versus risk and adversity, is a true high performer.

****

Sensory Efficiency

In Chapter 5, we discussed the concept of emotional efficiency, where you are able to accomplish a lot using little emotional support. A related concept is that of sensory efficiency, whereby your senses are able to experience high intensity feelings from a normal event.

Take two people eating the same apple-pie: one of them might be enjoying it much more than the other, even though they both have similar taste buds. How do I know that? Because I, myself, could enjoy the same apple-pie more when I am in good mood than when I am stressed.

It's easy to agree with me that being happy makes you enjoy things generally more than being depressed. In the apple-pie example, your overall mood has affected the pie taste because it affects all your senses in a general manner.

So if you're in a bad mood and you want to enjoy an apple-pie, you could make a conscious effort to decouple the apple-pie experience from your general disposition by forcing yourself to focus on the apple-pie.

With time and practice, you can focus on the apple-pie and improve your enjoyment of it even when you're in a good mood. Eventually, you can reach a state of sensory efficiency in which you are able to appreciate the apple-pie experience more than most common mortals.

With even more time and practice, you could conceivably attain a point where you focus your emotional energy on the apple-pie and use it to enhance the apple-pie flavor. So if you're happy, you will focus your happiness on the apple-pie and make it more tasty. That part looks easy; the difficult part is to use your negative energy from being angry or depressed to draw more enjoyment from the apple-pie. I must admit I am still learning how to do that.

The following table provides a summary of the apple-pie experience depending on the level of expertise of the taster in sensory efficiency:

Level	Description
Normal	Apple-pie taste varies according to general mood
Advanced	Apple-pie tastes sublime, no matter what the mood
Expert	Additional boost from positive emotions gets apple-pie taste to levels above the definition of sublime
Master	Additional boost from negative emotions gets apple-pie taste to levels above the definition of sublime

The apple-pie is just an example to illustrate the concept of sensory efficiency, which applies to any other food or sensory experience such as enjoying a nice perfume, holding the hand of your partner, a tennis match or even a sunset.

There are people who are sensory-inefficient, meaning that a lot of stimulus is required to cause enjoyment. Drug addicts, alcoholics and gamblers are examples of sensory-inefficient people always looking for the higher high.

On the other hand, the more sensory-efficient you are, the less you need a stimulant. Yogis who derive great joy just from staring at a tree for hours are highly efficient from a sensory perspective.

As you grow older and mature, you should strive to evolve in the direction of greater sensory efficiency.

****

72

TEAM YOU

Introduction: Your Team and You

There are a number of highly-remunerated professions that allow you to achieve great success without the need to manage a team: for example, you can be a great surgeon, a gifted trader, a brilliant attorney, a celebrity actor or a star consultant.

But in most professions, working solo will not help you achieve your full potential. And maximizing your added value means making your skills available outside the limited amount of time you are able to devote. It means leveraging your skillset through a team that can grow and reach many more people than you could on your own.

Concretely, almost everyone, including those in professions listed above, will need to manage a team. Managing people is being taught at all business schools and has been the focus of thousands of books. In this section, I will tackle the subject through a practical approach, ignoring the classical concepts that have become part of our culture, to focus instead on areas where my practical experience will provide valuable insights.

Before we delve into the nitty-gritty of managing your teams, let me share with you two such insights and let them become the guiding principles behind the chapters that follow:

- Having a team means you have power. Power is necessary to achieve your goals, but it also corrupts: the larger the organization you are managing, the more power you have and the more boost to your ego. You will need to channel all that power into achievement and remain humble. If you let power go to your head, you will be capable of the worst mistakes. Jesus Christ, possibly the world's greatest leader by number of followers, washed the feet of his disciples.

- Leading means managing energy. We saw in the previous section that emotion is the key source of energy in our life. Your team is a collection of people with their emotions and energy. Your job as a leader is to understand this energy flow and enhance it, direct it and manage it.

The next 6 chapters are dedicated to helping you improve your leadership:

Chapter one discusses your team members: who should be on your team, how to get the most productive team members, what are the mistakes to avoid when building your team.

Chapter two focuses on your team organization: how to best deploy the team in order to minimize friction and maximize output.

Chapter three is concerned with team leadership: how you can add value to the team by being helpful, yet nurturing, determined yet motivating. How to be a great leader.

Chapter four tackles the subject of team culture: how to build a corporate culture that encourages individual performance and teamwork, high output and creativity, achievement and constructive dissent.

Chapter five outlines my advice to encourage team growth: how to keep your teams constantly learning and growing, how to foster and handle ambition.

Chapter six reviews team follow-up: how to measure team performance, how to reward performance and foster loyalty, how to control the team to ensure compliance with corporate governance and ethics guidelines.

I have designed this whole section to be comprehensive: each chapter will cover my selection of best managerial practices in addition to my own personal insights and concepts not taught in business schools. By implementing the advice outlined in these chapters, you should be able to do an excellent job managing teams, even if you read or study nothing else.

Chapter 1: Team Members

After more than 5 years with Booz & Co, in the summer of 1995, I was in discussions with the management of BLOM Bank, the Lebanese banking giant, to join their senior management ranks and begin a reengineering of their branch network. I was meeting with the Chairman, Dr. Naaman Azhari, and the General Manager, Mr. Habib Rahal. Mr. Rahal, a results-driven practical man, began broaching the subject of the resources I would need in order to accomplish my mission:

- "What kind of team will you need to be working for you?"

- "I will need a team of 4-5 persons. They will need to be MBA-types, extremely analytical, the kind of persons that could be running the bank in 10-15 years."

Understandably, Mr. Rahal was not excited at the idea of concentrating all the bank's high-flyers in a single area:

- "What kind of backgrounds would they need to have? I can't empty the departments from their top people!"

- "They will need to have at most one year of experience."

- "You mean at least one year of experience?"

- "No, Mr. Rahal. I mean at most one year of experience. I want people I can teach, not people who already know. We will be reengineering, so we will be changing everything. People with experience may need to unlearn the usual way of doing business. People with no experience will approach the business with an open mind and will analyze rather than imitate. That's why they will need to be very smart."

As it turned out, the bank had just started a fast-track program for high-profile MBAs, so I was able to select 5 of them as my initial team. We were able to reengineer the branch network and they did become part of senior management 10-15 years later, but that's another story...

The "at most one year of experience" sound bite is sexy, but it doesn't really reflect my philosophy. What it does reflect is my need, at that time, for a team that had nothing to fall back on in case of failure and no loyalty except to the job I was leading.

Lest you believe MBA/analytical types are a good match for any job, let me tell you another story: This was in Indonesia, and I was working with my great friend Mark Hansen on an assignment for a bank in Jakarta. Every summer, Booz would hire a few interns for two months, so we were assigned a young Harvard MBA to help on our assignment. Since our assignment didn't require additional resources, we sat down with the bank's top management and made them an offer:

- "Look, we have this Harvard MBA student for two months. He is free of charge to you, but that doesn't mean he can't contribute. Is there any area of your business which you need to explore further, where we can direct him to provide insight?"

- "Well", said one of the senior managers, "we are experiencing a huge amount of staff turnover, especially among junior staff and new recruits. We'd really like to know why we have such a high turnover. Are our pay packages uncompetitive? Are our middle managers hard to work with? We really would like to know what the problem is!"

So Mark and I began focusing the new guy on staff turnover. After making all kinds of analyses of the characteristics of employees who had left, and after interviewing a large number of them, our trainee had a story to tell. So, we went back to the bank's senior management to announce the results of the study. It was Mark who broke the news:

- "It's actually pretty simple: The problem is one rule that your chairman has put in place about 3 years ago."

- "What rule?"

- "The rule that every bank employee must be a college graduate."

- "What's wrong with that rule?"

- "The problem is that many bank jobs are routine in nature and can get pretty boring pretty quickly. High-flying college graduates get frustrated at the slow pace of advancement and decide to quit. You need to recruit some lower-profile employees who are less in a hurry to advance."

Taking the two stories together, the morale is that your team will need to be diverse if it has to handle diverse tasks and you will need to be comfortable with people from all walks of life. As reported in the April 27, 2009 issue of Fortune Magazine, the CEO of Chinese conglomerate BYD figured out a way to make batteries cheaper than his Japanese competitors; While the Japanese use robots to build their batteries, he relied instead on low-cost migrant workers. So in the case of this company, it was uneducated migrant workers who provided the competitive advantage.

What kind of person you need depends on the job you need to accomplish. It also depends on the time you have available to train and supervise: At a certain point in my career, I insisted on having an inexperienced team because I needed full flexibility and I had the luxury of time to train the team. Later on in my career, I found I had much less time for interaction with a single individual, so I could no longer have inexperienced staff as direct reports.

Brian Dickie is the Booz & Co partner who recruited me into the firm and was the senior partner in charge of Asia-Pacific for much of my time there. He moved on from there to become the president of Booz for a period of time. Brian was known at the firm for his diligence and ambition and the people close to him always mentioned his singular focus on his teams and clients. While it would appear self-evident that a successful consultant should focus on team and clients, Brian did mark me with a quote he wrote in one of his memos: "Winners win", he said as he explained a recent wave of senior hires into the region.

Indeed, in most industries, winners tend to continue winning and mediocre performers rarely become winners. To succeed in a certain job, you need to have the corresponding aptitude, the correct attitude and be willing to invest the hard work. We have seen in preceding chapters that many people practice self-sabotage. If these people become part of your team, they will sabotage themselves and sabotage you and their other team members in the process.

Major consulting firms such as McKinsey, BCG and Booz typically have an "up or out" policy, meaning that each consulting employee is expected to either get promoted every 2-3 years or get told to leave the firm ("counseled out"). Such a model, which is probably only appropriate for very high intensity jobs such as consulting and investment banking, ensures that staff quality remains at a very high level.

While I definitely do not condone such extreme policies in other industries, I do believe you have to allow poor performers to get out of your team, to make room for new ones and to keep performance up to the standards. In consulting, as in the very top managerial positions, you need to make sure that the people at the top are winners. Otherwise, you will be (a) functioning at a lower level of performance as an organization and (b) keeping the high-performance future leaders from the opportunity to have a position where they could shine. It is also the reason why people should retire at retirement age.

However, in the vast majority of jobs, loyalty and reliability trump charisma, and cultivating loyalty means adopting "human" human resource policies. If your subordinates believe that you are ready to replace them as soon as you find someone better, they will also be looking to leave you at the first available opportunity. That's one reason why employee turnover is so high at major management consulting firms. In my experience, you need to surround yourself with a small core team of high-performance leaders and a larger team of competent, reliable managers and employees. In the following chapters, we will explore how to balance the requirement for high-performance with the requirement for having a stable team.

In building your team, you need to be aware that performance is a function of aptitude and energy. If your employee is spending 25% of his time looking at other job opportunities, he is only functioning at 75% energy. If he is spending another 25% of his time fighting with other team members, he is now working at 50% energy, so he is giving less output than someone who is 25% less able but 100% devoted.

I was once approached by a major bank located in a rich country of the Arabian Gulf for a senior position. The bank had just had a change of ownership and the new shareholders had tremendous ambition for their new acquisition. In particular, they had decided to replace all the key heads of businesses and key support areas at the same time. I was being approached for the position of "Head of Consumer Banking" and I had a shock when I learned that this was only one of the key positions they were looking to fill. I asked the CEO, who was himself a new hire:

- "I don't understand: this is not a new bank. Have you decided that all the top managers are bad? Is there no one you are not looking to replace?"

- "Well, the shareholders want a totally new team to take this place to a dramatically higher level of performance."

80

- "Are you aware that the logistics of incorporating all these new people, dealing with the resistance of the existing staff and getting everyone to work together might actually kill the added value of getting all these great people?"

- "I see your point, Elias, but our shareholders are adamant about all this change happening at the same time."

I did not take the position. A few months later, the bank did fill the position, along with some of the other senior positions it was looking to fill. The Human Resource Manager who had been the first of the new hires quit after less than a year on the job. The person who ended up taking the position that I was offered also quit after a few months on the job. The bank itself had to make a number of adjustments to recover its normal growth pattern.

One of the most prevalent management mistakes I have seen in my career is the tendency to discredit "old-style" employees in favor of newer, better-educated ones. A large number of top managers believe that a quick way to increase performance is to replace the former by the latter. This happens in companies undergoing restructuring or reengineering, in cases where one company acquires another and wants to get rid of most of the employees of the acquired company or in the case of a new general manager coming from the outside who wants to put her own team in place regardless of the competencies of the existing team. While a certain amount of "new blood" is positive and will promote a better performing culture, most people in a position of control in the cases above will overdo it. As a consultant promoting change and later as a banker involved in change management and in acquisitions, I have often found myself in a situation where I was advised to "junk the old and get new people". One of the secrets of my success has been that I chose, instead to "embrace the old while injecting a very limited number of new people". Let me tell you why:

- In cases of new management, acquisition, restructuring, etc., the existing staff is usually extremely insecure about their future. They **expect** their top management to discriminate against them. As a result, they will be spending a large amount of energy looking for jobs, fighting new people and new ideas and looking for/disseminating corporate gossip. If the top management does not immediately reassure them and embrace them, it will find them to be indeed lazy, unproductive and resistant to change. This is called a self-fulfilling prophecy! If, on the other hand, top management surprises them by adopting and embracing them (surprises create the strongest emotions), they will be taken over by positive emotions vis-à-vis their new management and will feel very guilty for having assumed they would be discriminated against. As a result, they will fight like tigers to further the cause of the new management.

- People have a tendency to underestimate other people's capacity to grow and to change. My experience has been that, given the proper incentive and motivation, people have a tremendous capacity to improve and to change. It is usually much more cost-effective to invest in training and motivation than to fire and hire.

- Corporations are not operating in a vacuum: they have customers, suppliers and regulators. These outside stakeholders are usually closer to the existing staff than to any new staff you are about to bring. In one bank, I have seen the general manager strive to gentrify branch staff and management, forgetting that the core customers of these branches identify more with the existing staff and would resent more upmarket and elitist branch representatives.

- "Winners win": before you showed up to run/acquire/restructure the corporation, it was a functioning entity with some degree of success. If you would like to improve on that success, the first step is to identify its elements, among which the key staff that are behind the success. For example, when we purchased a troubled bank in Egypt and turned it around, we were able to identify two extremely successful managers who had been behind its survival. After the acquisition, they became members of the top management team and continued to be successful in the better-capitalized, more resourceful organization: the post-acquisition entity.

- Top managers are often biased to prioritize process over results, excessively promoting new blood is one such bias: when I was working on developing a technology direction for a major bank in Thailand, I noticed that most banks there purchased most of their systems from IBM. In discussing the matter with IBM representatives, I was given the following explanation: "No IT manager ever got fired for choosing IBM!" While IBM is a great company, this quote opened my eyes to the importance of process in managerial decisions. In human resource issues, top managers are accountable to their boards and their shareholders. Displacing existing staff to hire "the best and the brightest" often confers to the manager an aura of toughness and drive even when the ultimate goal of performance would be better served by working with the existing staff.

Without new blood, on the other hand, an entity might be unable to achieve significant improvement. The key is how much new blood to

82

inject: When the BLOM Group purchased a bank in Egypt, I came over from Lebanon to run it and brought with me a team of 3 expatriates from Lebanon plus two specialists on a temporary basis. At that time, the Egyptian bank had about 450 employees of which about 10 were senior managers. As we grew the bank, we also recruited qualified resources from the Egyptian market, but this was a gradual effort.

In building my team, I tend to recruit at the bottom of the pyramid and promote from within. This demonstrates loyalty to my existing team, allows team members growth opportunities within the organization and minimizes misfits at the senior level. Sometimes, however, you do not have this luxury and you need to add selectively at the top layers from outside the organization.

In summary, building a team is a complex endeavor. Pure skills must be balanced with the right attitude. Loyalty and good fit are important attributes in evaluating a job applicant.

****

Team Members: Proactive and Disruptive

In the previous section, we discussed the existence of positive, negative and neutral in the structure of life and we reviewed practical applications of this phenomenon in emotional energy.

To review, positive energy makes you move forward and accomplish things in the direction you have already set for yourself, which is why I have called it proactive. However, if you want to change or alter your direction, you need negative, or disruptive energy.

You often hear a recruiter tell you he is looking for a team player, someone who will get along with the existing team. On the surface, the recruiter is right: you don't want a new recruit making trouble and creating tension in a high performance team. However, if the team is too homogeneous, many things may go wrong:

- People, convinced of their superiority as a team, may get complacent.

- The team, as a group, may filter out negative information and accept only good news. This phenomenon, called Groupthink was first identified by organizational thinker William Whyte and further expanded on by Yale and Berkeley professor Irving Janis. It is one reason behind the USA's low performance in the Vietnam war.

- Team decisions may become more consensus-oriented, and safe, meaning that difficult decisions are postponed. As a result, competitive moves can remain unanswered for a long time.

- Innovation is hampered due to satisfaction with the existing output.

- Sensing all of the above, bosses and/or outside customers may stop relying on the team for anything futuristic or controversial, leading to many projects being farmed out to outside consultants.

So if you want to protect your team in the long run, you must strike a balance between:

- Too much homogeneity leading to all the risks discussed above, and

84

- Too much conflict leading to your team wasting time and energy on finding common grounds versus moving forward.

A look at the world of politics provides ample examples of prospective/disruptive equilibrium in action:

- The one-party government in Tunisia could not survive a high unemployment climate in late 2010, and was ousted after popular riots and uprisings. Across the Mediterranean, in Greece, Spain and Portugal, similar or even higher unemployment numbers have been assimilated and accepted by the population. In a one-party system, people have only one party to blame for any problem that may arise; in a two-party system, people who don't like the party in power know they have an option to change it at the next election.

- On the other hand, government paralysis does occur when the two rival parties share the popular vote almost equally: in Iraq and Lebanon, for example, attempts to constitute a "unity government" take an inordinate amount of time and when such a government is created, it shies away from any major decision.

So if you see from time to time a talented element who might be different from others in your team or who may have a rebellious streak, give him a chance: he may actually have a good influence on the rest of the team.

****

Chapter 2: Team Organization

In my experience, there are five major traps that organizations tend to fall into when evolving:

1. Many managers try to maximize their marketability and measure their worth by how many people are reporting to them. Or they do not want their direct reports to complain about lack of staff. Or they are not held accountable to their staff expenses. In any case, they tend to overstaff their areas, which lowers service levels (extra staff creates its own extra work) and efficiency in the organization.

2. Organizations are often tailor-made to fit the personalities of top managers: the Head of Retail Banking is a great manager so let us give him his own IT and HR capabilities. Or the Head of IT is a great manager, so let us give him additional areas to manage under his CIO umbrella, such as electronic banking, the ATM network and product development. This works beautifully for a while, until the top managers involved leave, get promoted or retire and then the organization doesn't make sense any more.

3. In a bid to create team spirit and to ensure the involvement of all concerned areas, many organizations develop organization charts that are so complicated (matrix reporting, etc.) that they become impossible to decipher. With two or more direct bosses, the employee spends her time and energy reconciling the requirements of the various bosses and playing politics.

4. Managers with clout in the organization tend to take the blanket their way when a reorganization is taking place: Many managers try to increase the number of businesses or units they control through a reorganization while others may try to push risky businesses away from their responsibility. Ambitious young turks try to gobble as many responsibilities as they can while advocates of "plausible deniability" try to appear busy while shifting all real responsibilities to others. At the extreme, an institution that is so organized will experience total gridlock in some parts and no work done in others.

5. Many top managers are more concerned about personal power than about achievement. In an attempt to keep away any prospective challenger, they will often do one or both of the following: (1) give essentially the same responsibility to more than one person so that they can always pit one manager against another and (2) keep job responsibilities and job definitions very blurry so they are always able to

point the blame to the manager of their choice. I don't need to elaborate to convince you of how destructive these practices are.

Organizing is a science. For Booz&Co. and other consulting firms, it is a multibillion-dollar business. Consulting firms are in demand because they are aware of industry best practices and can provide unbiased recommendations.

Through my work at Booz&Co. and later on at BLOM Bank, I have been involved in a large number of reorganizations and have identified four grand principles to bear in mind when organizing/reorganizing:

- The first principle is CLARITY. This is a generally widely accepted principle of organizing with which most practitioners would agree.

- The second principle is VALUE ADDED. Again, part of the practitioner's arsenal, but generally not used very methodically.

- The third principle is OWNERSHIP. A word most people will agree with but not many will know how to put in practice.

- The fourth principle I will claim as my original contribution to organizational science. I'll call it MAXIMIZING THE ENERGY FLOW.

CLARITY

I distinctly remember the organization chart that had the most impact on me: It was the one unveiled by Hewlett-Packard's CEO Carly Fiorina after the merger between HP and Compaq. While I was personally generally favorable to the idea of the merger and to Carly Fiorina as a person, I was shocked at how complicated this organization chart was. As I was looking at it, I remember having two specific thoughts: My first thought was that Carly Fiorina was probably one of the most intelligent executives in business; my second was that she was probably too smart for her own good because very few people at HP and outside HP would be able to understand the chart. And if you can't understand what your job entails... your company is definitely in trouble!

In retrospect, Carly Fiorina's organization was probably suffering from pitfalls 3 and 5 outlined above: Fiorina probably wanted to involve everybody, at the expense of clarity and keep power in her hands by being able to assign the blame to the person of her choice. I would speculate that this chart was behind Fiorina's downfall: Fiorina, who joined HP in July 1999 as CEO after being named by Fortune Magazine "The most powerful woman in business" in 1998, acquired Compaq in 2002 and had to resign in early 2005. Her extremely successful successor Mark Hurd "abandoned many of Ms. Fiorina's radical organizational schemes and went back to a simple reporting structure based on product families", according to an April 15, 2007 article in the Wall Street Journal.

The first thing a job applicant asks from her prospective employer is an organization chart. If your prospective job is not well defined, you will be reluctant to take it: we have all heard all kinds of horror stories about abusive bosses, unclear responsibilities and over-competitive peers. Every executive wants to make her tenure a success story and the prerequisite for success is a job definition that provides clear roles and responsibilities.

VALUE ADDED

Simply put, the value-added approach considers that every action must add to the organization enough value to more than cover its cost. For example, if I am considering taking my team to a seminar in the Catskills, the value-added in terms of team motivation, new ideas and improved group dynamics should more than cover the costs of the seminar and the lost time and opportunities at the office. Typically, if I am organizing one of those a year, the value added will be easy to demonstrate; but if I am planning a seminar every month, the costs will likely clearly outweigh the benefits.

Ideally, an organization should be as flat as possible, meaning that it should have as few layers of middle management as possible. However, managers have a limited span of control, meaning that they can handle a limited number of direct reports. Beyond that number, some employees will be left unsupervised, which may lead to a loss of performance (although I have seen it sometimes lead to superior performance!). The value-added approach is instrumental to the decision of whether or not to add this extra layer: Say, for example, I was considering adding the position of regional manager so that the 50 branches of a restaurant don't all report to the Office of CEO. I would first look at what are the

88

requirements of these branches in terms of their needs from the CEO Office. Then, I would see how the CEO office keeps track of their performance and what it does to help them improve that performance. I would then check how much time this exercise is taking from the CEO Office and from the CEO herself. I would construct different scenarios with more or less supervision, as well as different types of supervision until I reach the best cost/benefit combination, which may or may not be adding a new management layer. One way of conducting this exercise is to have proponents and opponents of this new layer each present their argumentation.

Another great use of the value-added approach is to decide whether to have a committee and who to include as committee members. One way to undermine clarity in an organization is the overuse of committees. Committees are a great avenue to promote discussions and coordination, but they can also become dysfunctional. Typically, committees have too many members as many executives view their membership in a committee as a source of prestige, regardless of whether or not their presence adds value to the committee. The proliferation of committees and their attendant meetings has become so severe in the corporate world that a word -meetingitis- has been coined in the English language to describe the affliction of having to attend so many meetings that you can't get your work done!

When I took over as CEO of BLOM Bank Egypt for the second time, one of the first decisions I had to make was presented to me by Talal, the Assistant Managing Director for Support Areas. I had been Talal's mentor for most of his professional life, so he pretty much knew how I would respond to his inquiry:

- "Boss, what are you going to do about the IT Steering Committee?"

- "What's that?"

- "It's a committee that meets once a week and has about thirty members from all areas of the bank. Its meetings take hours."

- "Let's cancel it for now and see what happens."

A few days after canceling that committee, I learned that the bank had a problem in processing electronic debits coming from its card processor. The card operations area blamed IT, and IT blamed the processor and no progress was being made. So I decided to have a weekly meeting involving operations and IT. The meetings were very effective and, as we started to get a handle on the problem, I decided to include Audit, to

89

make sure they were aware of the new procedures we were putting in place. With Audit, we had to include Risk Management who are concerned with tracking operational risk and Financial Control because we had some reconciliation issues with the accounts affected by the cards. With all these participants, we had about 50% of the previous IT Steering Committee roster, but everyone in this committee had a purpose and added value. This committee became the replacement for the IT Steering Committee: one half the participants and much shorter sessions, but twice as effective.

OWNERSHIP

The above example is also great to describe the concept of ownership, or rather the lack of it. The initial problem was one of processing electronic debits at the bank. The card operations area was blaming IT. IT was blaming the outside company that processed our card transaction. In the meantime, we had many transactions going to the wrong place and some customers being furious. What the situation needed was an owner.

An owner is someone you will hold responsible for a certain situation, no matter whose fault it is and no matter whether it is technically his job to fix it or not. If someone throws garbage into your room, you will have it removed before you sleep. It doesn't matter that you're not the one who put the garbage there: if you don't remove it, you'll have to sleep with it. It doesn't matter that you have a cleaning lady who is supposed to remove it; if she is on vacation, you'll have to do the job yourself.

There is always an owner in an organization: In the card-processing example above, the two owners were Talal, because all the concerned departments were reporting to him and me since I was the CEO. I was obviously not pleased to be the owner of such a problem when the managers and employees of the concerned departments were not really working to solve it, so my first act in the committee was to select an owner:

- "The cards operations department is responsible for the resolution of this problem. I want a plan for how you will take care of it."

Not too pleased, the head of card processing answered:

- "But it is not our fault if IT is processing the files wrong."

90

- "In every organization, there are owners and enablers. IT is an enabler and you are the owner. If IT fails to deliver what you need, you implement a workaround, but you don't let something wrong happen. You are the custodian of good customer service when it comes to cards and I will hold you accountable for anything having to do with cards. I will help you, however, in getting IT to respond to your requests but we all have to understand that you are driving this initiative."

With these words began the process of resolving our issues.

As we said, when there is no owner, the CEO becomes the ultimate owner. The key is to assign ownership at a level in the organization where something can be done effectively and in a timely fashion.

Any one who has worked at a bank has experienced the constant conflict between business development and credit: while business development officers are interested in growing the business, credit analysts care mainly about loan portfolio quality. This translates often into the former bringing files they feel strongly about only to see the latter reject because they view them as risky. Mort used to be an influential credit risk analyst at a medium-sized bank and used to be called unflattering names by most branch managers who dealt with him. A few years later, the chairman of the bank decided to give Mort responsibility for the management of a branch. When Mort became a branch manager, he became the credit department's worst enemy: from overly careful, he metamorphosed into a business courting adventurer advocating what was viewed as risky loans that were all rejected by his former home, the credit department. These kinds of true stories lead most people to advocate that business development and credit risk analysis be separated by Chinese walls. Most New York bank training programs include the famous phrase: "Aggressive marketing, conservative lending" and emphasize the need to look at a credit risk with objective eyes.

In my organizational work at BLOM Bank, I have often been confronted with the dilemma of how to structure a credit function: for example, should the head of retail credit be reporting to the head of retail banking or to the head of risk management? My preference has always been to keep all functions under a business head (so the first option), but in many of BLOM's subsidiaries, other managers have successfully argued for the second option on the basis of avoiding conflict of interest. So, after about 15 years with BLOM and seeing both options at work, I can truthfully report that the configuration with the highest quality of credit was the first, despite its conflict of interest issue. Why? Because the business owner cared about the quality of his business and because the CEO could hold only one person responsible for the growth and quality of the business. In the other case, the infighting between business and credit led to lower quality files being approved with each side blaming the other for the problems.

Again, and this is my experience: avoiding conflict of interest is good, but making sure there is an owner you can go to is better.

The long-time Chairman and key success person at BLOM Bank, Dr. Naaman Azhari recently wrote his memoirs and concluded them with his ten tenets of successful bank management. In one of them, he states that the best bank ownership structure is one where the top manager is also a key shareholder, so he is motivated to manage for the long-term while simultaneously not having a controlling stake, meaning that he can be removed by other shareholders in case of poor performance. It strikes me as a valid principle for all kinds of organizations.

MAXIMIZING THE ENERGY FLOW

Each one of us is a combination of competing forces: our left-brain values consistency, routine and reliability while our right brain is concerned with creativity, play and emotional fulfillment. Competing energy flows are part of every organism: In much of African history, there has been a conflict between farmers and herders. The farmers want to cultivate land and need the water for irrigation; they would like to see animals as far away from their land as possible. The herders are competing for the same resources: they need grass and water for their herds. In any corporation, you can see tension between "old-schoolers" who want to preserve the status quo and newcomers who see new opportunities and want to change things. Or between business developers for whom the sky is the limit and risk managers who want to steer away from anything remotely risky.

As a manager, you need to acknowledge all the energy flows inside your organization. After you have identified them, you need to put in place the infrastructure that will make the most of these energy flows:

92

- The first thing you need to do is identify the main thrust of your organization, its (and your) main objective. You then need to make sure that the most powerful energy within the organization is aligned with this main objective. Let's call this the positive energy.

- The next step is to make sure that there is a competing and opposite energy in the organization. This is what provides creativity, renewal, accountability and prudence in the organization. We'll call it the negative energy.

- Positive and negative energy flows cannot be equal, or there will be gridlock. One energy flow has to be stronger in order to move the organization, but the other side must be strong enough to act as a safeguard and renewal mechanism.

Successful governments work in the above model:

- The party that wins elections gets to govern, and the losing party is in the opposition.

- When the two sides are almost equal in power, there is gridlock. That has been the case recently in Ukraine, Palestine and Lebanon.

- However, when the opposition is muzzled, the government turns into a dictatorship where human rights are suppressed and improvements become scarce. Eventually, the country goes into self-destruct mode, as was the case with the Soviet Union, Nazi Germany, prewar Japan, etc.

Indeed, it is interesting to note that almost every democratic country in the world has evolved into a two-party (or two-coalition) system of government. Attempts to create a "third way" are usually short-lived and unsuccessful: think of Ross Perot and Ralph Nader in the USA and Francois Bayrou in France. Sometimes, the leadership and constituents of the two opposite poles change, but the polarization is still among two groups: Should the Tea Party in the US be able to acquire significant traction, it will eventually take the place of one of the two other large parties.

But we have digressed, so let's get back to our main subject: One of your main tasks as a manager is to make sure that energy flows healthily in the organization: meetings get all the issues and opinions aired, but do not result in stalemates. Decisions are carefully considered, yet made and implemented with passion. There are enough (but not too many) "No" persons in the organization, but their "No"s are constructive. And

93

through it all, everyone still has the drive and motivation to play her role whether as "Yes" person or "No" person.

****

Organizational Imbalance: The Subprime Crisis of 2008

Unless you are reading this book decades after I wrote it, you must have heard and been affected by the financial crisis of 2008, which led to the failure of mammoth investment bank Lehman Brothers and to the loss of millions of jobs worldwide. The initial catalyst for the crisis was the investment on the part of many financial institutions into packaged mortgage loans of dubious quality called subprime.

These loans were called subprime prior to their turning bad and putting thousands of banks in trouble. They were called subprime because they did not fulfill the classical prudence criteria that banks look for when providing housing loans: a decent down payment, a borrower who has enough income to pay his mortgage bill and have about two thirds of his paycheck left for his other expenses, a good credit history, etc. Not only that, but many of these loans were made with very low teaser rates that would reset after 1, 2, 3 years or more. Since interest rates at the time the loans were made were at historical lows, it was almost assured that loan repayment amounts would drastically increase upon reset, meaning a huge problem would ensue for the borrower and his bank.

Why did bankers make these loans? My answer is that bankers didn't, mathematicians did: some quantitative geniuses figured that, by charging higher interest rates on these loans, they would be profitable even if the default rate on them was substantially higher. What the genius mathematicians didn't see was that if default rates went up substantially and required banks to foreclose on many properties simultaneously, the price of houses would come down causing major losses for the banks and encouraging other borrowers, whose houses were now worth less than their mortgages, to also default! That vicious circle seems evident and some bankers, such as Jamie Dimon of JP Morgan Chase, had seen it and steered clear from it. So why did it happen?

In giving you my own explanation for the subprime crisis, allow me to backtrack and signal a coincidence that holds a key to my answer: In the few years leading to the subprime crisis, banks had been subjected to major organizational requirements with the objective of improving corporate governance and risk management. To wit:

- In June 2004, the Basel Committee on Banking Supervision, an institution created by the central bank governors of the Group of Ten nations, issued the famous Basel II accord which requires banks to set up large and powerful risk management departments to monitor and control credit, market and operational risks at banks. These departments theoretically report directly to the board, meaning they can conceivably block CEO decisions. While Basel II was first issued in June 2004, most banks began feeling its impact from 2006 onward.

- A little bit earlier, corporate governance had become a new management trend and a number of initiatives were put in place at banks worldwide to improve control over management: audit departments reporting directly to the board of directors, a limitation on the number of executive directors, etc.

- Around the same period, new departments called compliance were created inside the banks to ensure compliance with all kinds of regulations such as anti-money-laundering, consumer lending guidelines, investment guidelines, etc.

- In many cases, the regulator multiplied control requirements: for example, I have seen banks with an IT security team located in IT, another in audit and a third in risk management!

The impact of all these requirements should have been to increase controls and make banks more transparent and prudent. However, because of the intense and sudden character of their implementation, I submit that their actual impact was as follows:

- Tremendously increase operating costs at banks as all these new departments not only cost money, but also provide additional work for other areas of banks

- Add new staff with low banking experience: since all these banks had to create all these functions at the same time, they had no choice but to raid other industries for talent to fill all the available positions

- Dilute ownership as responsibility for control became split among many areas: business, audit, compliance, risk management, the CEO and the board.

So what happened? Some math geeks devised this financing plan and got rating agencies (Moody's and S&P, themselves challenged in their staffing due to competition from banks in recruiting quality talent) to provide a high rating for the related paper. Banks, under pressure to make profits in this high cost environment were all too happy to purchase high-yielding paper that had high safety ratings. Risk managers would look like fools if they questioned the agency ratings, so eventually everybody jumped on the bandwagon. Of course, the fact that so many banks were now offering these loans made them more vulnerable to a system collapse, but now Moody's and S&P couldn't go back and downgrade the paper, as they would lose credibility and cause a system collapse. Instead, it was the high default rate by customers that did cause the collapse.

It would seem counterintuitive to reduce oversight in a time of crisis, but I would advocate rationalizing controls on banks to ensure increased ownership (fewer oversight departments, more responsibility to the business) and simplified regulation (focus on the really dangerous items).

****

Chapter 3: Team Leadership

If you ask the board of directors of a company what the purpose of appointing a manager is, you should get the same answers as asking the manager's subordinates why they need a boss. Taken from both these perspectives, a manager, to my knowledge, has four core leadership functions:

- She must be an efficient energy manager, making good use of the team's energy.

- She is an example that people in the company can look up to.

- She is a decision-maker.

- She must be able to help her subordinates overcome difficulties and succeed.

Each of these core functions has its secrets. I would like to share my experience and the secrets I have uncovered.

ENERGY MANAGEMENT

Like the conductor of an orchestra, the manager is in charge of producing great music out of many team members working together. Output requires energy, so if you want to obtain the best output, you need to work on the energy: using it, developing it, channeling it.

Each member of your team comes with a certain amount of energy or drive; some people are full of ideas and initiatives and others are more subdued, but everyone has something that you can build on:

- Let's say that I am interested in reducing expenses, increasing the number of locations of my company and recruiting new people for one of our new offices. I haven't made my plans known yet, but, out of the blue, Tim, the auditor, approaches me with his concerns about the excessive cost of office supplies in the organization. I could tell Tim "Thanks for the tip, Tim, I'll make sure we look at this when we start working on expenses", and that's probably the classical way of dealing with Tim. A better way, in my view, would be "Great, Tim. I was planning on looking at expenses sooner or later, so why don't you get deeper into the subject and give me a detailed report on the office supply situation ASAP". With this, I have used Tim's natural inclination and drive to push my agenda faster. Plus, Tim is probably going to work better and faster than anyone else I could have put on the subject.

- Every day, I try to scout who on my team is passionate about some initiative and I try to see how to involve that person with his pet project. By playing with the prioritization and timing of my own goals, I can make great use of the energy of my subordinates. So, I try to accommodate every "I think we should..." or "we need to look at..." with the general goals I have set for myself and for the company.

- Of course, I still need to get my key initiatives implemented, even if they have no unprompted champion! Plus, it is a real challenge to deal with the likes of Patty: Patty is a great worker, full of energy and smiles; but she always has these "great suggestions" that are not so great. There are many ways to handle a Patty without killing her motivation. The one that works best for me is to quickly shoot down Patty's initial idea in a rational, calm and analytical manner and then suggest another initiative that has a similar goal and that will keep Patty focused on what I want her to do. That way, I still get to use Patty's energy while coaching her on how to fulfill her goals.

One way of sabotaging yourself by killing a subordinate's energy is called "micromanagement". Micromanagement, when a boss gets involved in the smallest details, more often than not, results in employee demotivation and disenchantment. Micromanaged employees typically lack initiative. I make it a rule to provide my team with only as much support as they seem to require. I will typically explain the end result that I am looking for and wait for questions to emerge. If I feel that the team member is confident about how to achieve the results, I will not get involved in the process. If I feel that the team member requires additional guidance, I will provide it. Of course, I will monitor progress on a regular basis.

Monitoring progress is an essential part of energy management: if your team is doing well, you should voice your encouragement. If not, you should step in and show the way forward; going so far as performing certain tasks yourself, leading by example. In no circumstance, should you make disparaging or derogatory comments about what the subordinate has chosen to do: that's another way of killing his initiative.

There are instances, however, where I will express anger at a subordinate:

that's when he undertakes initiatives that are going totally counter to the direction I want the organization. Then, I don't mind killing his initiative: no action is much better than destructive action. For example, if I am trying to improve customer service, and someone introduces a new process loaded with bureaucracy with inefficient controls, I will not hesitate to ridicule the initiative and its champion, sending the message that customer service is not something we should tamper with lightly. Lazy proposals that result in major inefficiency are always sure to get me worked up. That being said, these instances of brutal confrontation should be extremely rare, remain within acceptable professional boundaries and be followed by intense coaching sessions with the concerned subordinate.

Your team will include some close subordinates, maybe as few as 3, possibly as many as 20. These people are working for you and your success is their success. On the principle that "two heads are better than one" (and therefore twenty heads are better than one), I am usually very transparent about my concerns and my goals. I don't bog down my subordinates with all my work, but I will share my greatest issues and see if one of them has a solution. I do it informally, without scheduling special meetings, and without spending more than five minutes to describe the problem. If I don't see a person that day, I will not call her to run the problem past her, I just go with the flow, being transparent with whoever happens to be with me at a specific point in time. I find that, very often, what looks to me like a very complicated problem ends up with an easy solution I had not thought about. That's part of leveraging the energy of the team.

A related habit I recommend you develop is to develop simple messages that you can communicate to all your staff, whether they are part of your close circle or not. The purpose of hammering these simple messages is to ensure everyone is working in the same direction. Working in different directions is at best a waste of time and at worst an exercise in sabotage.

We saw in the first section that energy comes from emotion, and emotion is a result of transactions. Your team will come with a certain energy, but it is your role as a manager to maintain and increase this energy. This is what is called motivating your team.

Traditional management scholars look at motivation from the perspective

100

of reward and punishment. In a recent article in the American Economic Review, authors James Andreoni, William Harbaugh and Lise Vesterlund argue that rewards and punishment are complementary; they are two sides of the same coin, and you cannot have one without the other. This makes sense to me philosophically: assume a world of no punishment, only rewards. Lack of reward would then automatically become punishment! And vice versa, in a world of only punishment, the lack of punishment becomes a reward!

If your approach to motivation is to implement the best possible incentive and reward system, you will never reach your full potential as a motivator: punishments and rewards are the cherry on the cake of motivating your employees, they are not the cake! Building a truly motivated team requires you to instill in your people a sense of fighting for survival, a sense of building huge accomplishments and to give their work great meaning. "Only the paranoid survive" was Andy Grove's maxim when he was the CEO of Intel.

Emotions trump rationality every time. Adolf Hitler was able to rise to power and get his people to commit atrocious acts by playing on nationalistic pride. Elsewhere in the world at various times in history, extremist leaders of all religions have used religious affiliation and emotions to get their followers to accomplish irrational and hateful actions.

In 1943, leading human behaviorist Abraham Maslow identified what he called a "hierarchy of needs". Under his theory, which is now the basis for management teachings at business schools, human beings have five levels of basic needs operating in hierarchy, meaning that you need to satisfy the most urgent needs first before moving on and also meaning that once you have satisfied the basic needs, the higher-level needs become the important motivators. The basic needs are, in order of urgency, physiological needs (food, shelter, etc.) and safety needs. The higher-level needs, also in order of urgency, are the need for belonging, esteem and self-actualization. While there are similarities between my point and Maslow's hierarchy of needs, I would like to emphasize that I am talking about emotions, while Maslow is talking about needs. While emotions may originate from needs, they can then have a life and potency of their own.

Being the purchasing manager of a car company is hardly the world's most exciting job. Yet, that was Jose Ignacio Lopez de Arriortua's job at General Motors in the early 1990s when he became one of the most colorful management icons of his time. "Inaki", as he was nicknamed, was credited for saving about $4 billion in expenses at the car company while pushing its suppliers to near bankruptcy. He used to call his inner circle "the warriors" and you can bet they were the most motivated people on the planet. However, his outsized ambition took him too far and he was later accused by GM of stealing trade secrets and taking them with him to his new job at Volkswagen.

Whether we like it or not, we are currently living in an era of superlatives: if you view your job as just a job, and if you convey that view to your team, you will never be more than mediocre. This doesn't mean you and your team need to work 20 hours a day, it just means you need to approach the job with fervor, as if your life depended on it.

In other words, your team needs to be entrepreneurial: spend the maximum amount of time and energy on business issues and business development and the least possible amount of time on bureaucracy and noncore issues. This is easy to do in small organizations where everyone does everything, and more difficult in large organization which become political as they grow. One way to energize these large organizations is to break down some of the divisions into smaller cells that function entrepreneurially and almost independently.

In this context of creating fervor and energy, it is not too difficult to understand my skepticism toward target and goal setting: Suppose I am in sales of airplanes and I set myself a target of 10 planes per year. Does it mean that if I am able to sell 20 planes in a particular year, I will stop at 10? Or 12 so I am not too far from my budget? Many organizations spend an inordinate amount of time and effort on budgeting, only to see their business units become more bureaucratic and stifled. Ideally, budgeting should remain a small exercise, intended for management to forecast results and to evaluate individual performance (by comparing what an individual has done versus others who have been in the same position). Targets should be treated as guidelines that are not set in stone.

Besides, the concept of target implies that the boss is more motivated to achieve results than her subordinate, which is part of the reason she sets

102

targets for him. I question this premise and my experience is that, in well-motivated teams, the subordinate is at least as committed to results as her boss.

When I am asked about my plans for the next year or the next five years, I often respond: "The maximum I can", and I mean it. I set no limit for my goals and try my best. I use competitor performance and benchmarks to see if my process is correct: if a competitor is able to outperform my team, it means I need to improve my organization.

ROLE MODEL

Technically, a good manager could get away with working very few hours as long as her subordinates work very hard. For a period of almost a year, I was able to run a bank in Egypt while spending only 3 nights a week in the country! And we were able to achieve dramatic improvement. However, before you run for the golf course, you should know that, in practice, if you goof off, your team will goof off.

Your employees look at you as a role model: you are the key player in their professional life, and possibly in their overall life. As they grow in the organization, they might one day be promoted to fill your shoes and therefore you are offering them an example of how to behave. Plus, if your behavior got you where you are, they have reason to believe that by acting like you they will also be able to move up the ladder.

If you are following the "survival" mode of motivation described just earlier, you need to walk the walk: you have to be as committed as you want your team to be. Your job should be a calling, not just a place to spend 9 to 5 at. You need to show how driven you are, not necessarily by working very long hours, but by being intense, avoiding chitchat and other timewasters and following up on all subject of importance. Taking the job seriously (or not) is contagious and it starts at the top: if you act careless or tolerate carelessness, you can be sure that your organization will become careless.

You can be intense without being anal, careful and efficient but also smiling and relaxed. You don't need to freak out your employees to show your commitment to the business. You also need to project an image of competence and self-confidence; being relaxed is a great way to project that image.

Most importantly, be humble: don't let the power go to your head. You need to be achievement-oriented, not power-oriented. Otherwise, your team, taking their cues from you, will also become little monsters with their own subordinates or fight among themselves for power and positioning. Personally, I come down very hard on anyone on my team whose personal agenda diverges from the interest of the business.

Certainly as a leader, you must be honest and fair and apply the highest degree of integrity. If you are human, you are bound to have favorites among your employees. This is especially true if you are using emotion to power your team, as explained previously. You need to be aware of that fact to make sure you don't discriminate.

DECISION-MAKING

As a leader, you are expected to make decisions. While this sounds obvious, I cannot tell you how many executives I have met who are afraid of making decisions.

Of course, making decisions involves more than just making decisions: you have to be able to own up to your decision when questioned by a higher up or when events later show the decision to have been wrong. A good leader will make decisions after reviewing major aspects of an issue or agree to the recommendations of a subordinate. Whatever the initial source of the decision, the leader should consider it her own and defend it.

The quickest way to lose the respect of your team is to hold them solely accountable for a decision that was made on your watch. "Plausible deniability" may have its place in international espionage, but it is not an effective management tool.

Many managers like decision-making by consensus. For them, it is the best way to ensure all the concerned parties buy into the decision and

104

therefore deploy their best to implement it. I have noticed that this type of decision-making is very popular in the Far East. However, my own experience with consensus-based decision-making has largely been negative:

- It is a very inefficient way of making decisions, wasting the time of sometimes dozens of people.

- I have noticed that this type of decision-making tends to produce decisions that are extremely watered-down, as participants tend to form consensus around the lowest common denominator.

Consensus-based decision-making will never produce large initiatives or major change and is probably best reserved for noncontroversial projects requiring a lot of collaboration.

HELP

Part of the classical view of management is that the boss, the owner of the business, must set objectives and priorities for the subordinates to achieve. In case of nonperformance, the boss may remove or reallocate employees to get the proper person in the proper job.

While this view is partly correct, it fails to take into consideration that, in well-motivated teams, the subordinates are the real "owners" of their business. In fact, the success of the franchise concept and the proliferation of profit-sharing schemes in the workplace are a testament to the power of the "partner" empowered subordinate.

So if we twist the view and make the subordinate the owner of his portion of the business, what becomes the role of the boss?

- To ensure coordination among various subordinates and other stakeholders. This involves making the decisions that can favor one constituent over another for the greater good of the institution.

- To ensure all the team members are equally motivated and working to their best abilities.

- To be a great role model for his various subordinates.

- To help those team members who are not able to function at a high level of performance.

This last task is significant: it implies that the boss is also a help resource for his subordinates. It means that the boss is not some employer with people working FOR him; he is rather working for his subordinates, helping them achieve their goals.

So if you catch yourself saying to someone: "I have x number of people working for me", I have both good and bad news for you:

- The bad news is that you are not a great manager

- The good news is that you have the potential to greatly improve the performance of your organization. How? By becoming more humble and seeing yourself as a resource for your empowered employees rather than as a ruler with a team of helpers.

CONCLUSION

I came up with this model of team leadership involving four core functions based on my experience as a manager and working with other managers. Later on, I found the model to be uncannily strong in explaining a number of successes or failures of leadership in the corporate world.

****

The Leadership Model and Steve Jobs

Few people will dispute the assertion that Steve Jobs is one of the greatest managers of all time. What is more important to me, however, is the fact that he is a poster boy for the concept that leadership skills can be acquired over time.

Steve Jobs was certainly a born visionary with a knack for predicting what products could prove successful, and he also was fortunate to find himself in the right place at the right time. Let's also agree that he is a very charismatic marketer/communicator.

All of the above factors combined account for his early success at Apple and would have been sufficient to secure for him a place in history. However, by his own recognition and that of his early backers, these innate gifts were not sufficient to qualify him for the role of CEO in the early days at Apple: he was considered immature and unruly, which is why an outsider, Mike Scott, was brought in as CEO in 1978, two years after Apple was founded.

In 1983, Apple's board felt new management was needed and John Sculley was brought in from Pepsico to become CEO. At that point, Steve Jobs was an executive board member at Apple and was a key proponent of recruiting Sculley, luring him with the famous: "Do you want to sell sugar water for the rest of your life, or do you want to come with me and change the world?"

Two years later, the management styles of Jobs and Sculley began to clash and Jobs was relieved from his duties as head of the Macintosh Division, amid claims by his detractors that he had become dysfunctional.

Later on, Jobs resigned from Apple completely and pursued a number of successful ventures. Apple, on the other hand, quickly deteriorated and was considered in 1996 by many analysts beyond saving.

In 1996, Jobs joined Apple as CEO and did an outstanding job in resuscitating the company and taking it to a level of uncontested leadership among organizations.

Steve Jobs went from being rejected by the company he founded to one of the world's greatest leaders. He is definitely someone worth listening to.

I have taken excerpts from an interview Steve Jobs did with Fortune Magazine in 2008, and placed them in the appropriate buckets of our leadership model. As you will see, they do a good job of confirming not only the model but also other concepts of the book.

ENERGY MANAGEMENT

"When I hire somebody really senior, competence is the ante. They have to be really smart. But the real issue for me is, Are they going to fall in love with Apple? Because if they fall in love with Apple, everything else will take care of itself. They'll want to do what's best for Apple, not what's best for them, what's best for Steve, or anybody else.

"It's not about pop culture, and it's not about fooling people, and it's not about convincing people that they want something they don't. We figure out what we want. And I think we're pretty good at having the right discipline to think through whether a lot of other people are going to want it, too. That's what we get paid to do.

"So you can't go out and ask people, you know, what the next big [thing.] There's a great quote by Henry Ford, right? He said, 'If I'd have asked my customers what they wanted, they would have told me "A faster horse."'

"We all had cellphones. We just hated them, they were so awful to use. The software was terrible. The hardware wasn't very good. We talked to our friends, and they all hated their cellphones too. Everybody seemed to hate their phones. And we saw that these things really could become much more powerful and interesting to license.

ROLE MODEL

"We've got really capable people at Apple. I made Tim [Cook] COO and gave him the Mac division and he's done brilliantly. I mean, some people say, 'Oh, God, if [Jobs] got run over by a bus, Apple would be in trouble.' And, you know, I think it wouldn't be a party, but there are really capable people at Apple. And the board would have some good choices about who to pick as CEO. My job is to make the whole executive team good enough to be successors, so that's what I try to do.

"When you hire really good people you have to give them a piece of the business and let them run with it. That doesn't mean I don't get to kibitz a lot. But the reason you're hiring them is because you're going to give them the reins. I want [them] making as good or better decisions than I would. So the way to do that is to have them know everything, not just in their part of the business, but in every part of the business.

108

DECISION-MAKING

"Apple is a $30 billion company, yet we've got less than 30 major products. I don't know if that's ever been done before. Certainly the great consumer electronics companies of the past had thousands of products. We tend to focus much more. People think focus means saying yes to the thing you've got to focus on. But that's not what it means at all. It means saying no to the hundred other good ideas that there are. You have to pick carefully.

"We've had one of these before, when the dot-com bubble burst. What I told our company was that we were just going to invest our way through the downturn, that we weren't going to lay off people, that we'd taken a tremendous amount of effort to get them into Apple in the first place -- the last thing we were going to do is lay them off. And we were going to keep funding. In fact we were going to up our R&D budget so that we would be ahead of our competitors when the downturn was over. And that's exactly what we did. And it worked. And that's exactly what we'll do this time.

"We had a big debate inside the company whether we could do that or not. And that was one where I had to adjudicate it and just say, 'We're going to do it. Let's try.' The smartest software guys were saying they can do it, so let's give them a shot. And they did.

HELP

"We've got 25,000 people at Apple. About 10,000 of them are in the stores. And my job is to work with sort of the top 100 people, that's what I do. That doesn't mean they're all vice presidents. Some of them are just key individual contributors. So when a good idea comes, you know, part of my job is to move it around, just see what different people think, get people talking about it, argue with people about it, get ideas moving among that group of 100 people, get different people together to explore different aspects of it quietly, and, you know - just explore things.

"My job is to not be easy on people. My job is to make them better. My job is to pull things together from different parts of the company and clear the ways and get the resources for the key projects. And to take these great people we have and to push them and make them even better, coming up with more aggressive visions of how it could be.

****

Chapter 4: Team Culture

At Company A, executives are extremely well paid. In addition, they get many fringe benefits such as open expense accounts, low interest loans, frequent seminars in exotic locations, etc. There, people who watch expenses are described as "accountants", a very derogatory term at the company. In their leisure time, executives are expected to have a very active social life with abundant networking. They are expected to look rich and flamboyant, be noticed and to make an impression in society. At work, major deals are encouraged; day-to-day operations are not a key management priority.

Company B is in the same business. Its executives are fairly compensated, without any excess. Expenses are tightly controlled and the superfluous doesn't exist. Executives are generally competent, but low-key. They don't go out much and would probably never make the cover of a society magazine. Should they become too visible, they would get an admonition from the chairman. At work, people are expected to excel at day-to-day operations and focus on pristine customer service. Major deals are viewed with suspicion and emphasis is on internal growth.

The two companies are major competitors but they have very different ways of approaching the business. Each company has its own set of written and unwritten values and approaches to business; it is what is commonly known as a corporate culture.

Within the same corporation, there are usually a number of different subcultures that correspond to the various entities in the organization. For example, the accounting department at company A, partly because it is not viewed as the most prestigious area of the organization, will probably have a much different culture than the rest of the company. I have called team culture the culture you want to instill in your own team.

It is extremely important to have a team culture: without it, teamwork is not fully coordinated and there is no real team spirit. Over time, if you don't consciously work on putting in place the proper team culture, the team will develop its own culture anyway, and it may not be what you had in mind.

110

Creating a team culture is simple: you just have to praise and reward team behavior that is consistent with the culture you want and at the same time discourage and punish any behavior that is inconsistent with that culture. Over time, the team will have a new culture. Depending on how much resistance you encounter, the transition period to the new culture will be longer or shorter. So, in creating a culture, you have two main issues to consider:

- What kind of culture do you want in place?

- How to overcome resistance to the new culture.

THE RIGHT CULTURE

Many parts of the right culture are particular to your personal style, your organization strategy, the type of products you sell, etc. However, in my experience, there is a common foundation you can build on whatever your style or type of organization. I will therefore focus on this foundation, which is composed of three parts:

1. Building the right "winner aura"

If you want your team members, your customers and even you to believe in your team and invest in it, you need everyone to perceive it as a "winning team". When I was studying at Columbia, the local football team, the "Columbia Lions", had a dismal game performance, which put it squarely at the bottom of the Ivy League teams. I remember my classmates going to Lions matches, not expecting any victory and not taking the team seriously. That is the opposite of the image and self-confidence you want for your team.

How to build this "winner aura"? For Booz & Co., like many major consulting firms, this is a paramount issue: New teams are deployed to new client sites, often for short periods of time, at very substantial fees for the client and are often met with a lot of skepticism by existing client staff. Both team and client must be convinced very quickly that the Booz team can add tremendous value; way above and beyond what the client could do on its own. A great tool for accomplishing that is what is called in Booz terminology "quick hits".

"Quick hits", also called "low-hanging fruit", are initiatives that can be completed relatively quickly and easily and yield great results for the organization. In a typical assignment, we would try to identify these potential hits early, then put them in place quickly to build confidence in the team.

The best example I have to offer on this topic is actually something I have done after I left Booz: I had just been hired by BLOM Bank and my first assignment was to reengineer their branch network. I expected that I would need at least one year before the first reengineered branch could be showcased, as the effort required major IT overhaul. Plus, the assignment had some detractors who didn't want to change the status quo and many skeptics who viewed me then as an idealist who couldn't get practical results. And this skepticism could easily rub off on my team, which was composed of very smart, but young and inexperienced individuals. I definitely needed some "quick hits".

After a review of branch operations, I found it odd that BLOM branches, in line with most other Lebanese bank branches at the time, closed for customer business at 12:30 pm, while branch employees finished work at 2 pm. It struck me as peculiar that the branches would have all their employees present inside for an hour and a half while the customers could not be serviced. Upon investigating the issue further, I was told that they needed this hour and a half in order to close their books and reconcile their cash. I knew from experience that you don't need more than half an hour to do these things, so I investigated further and, when learning that this was the practice at all Lebanese banks, I suspected that it was a remnant of the 1960s when banks were not fully computerized and many books were kept by hand. So, I asked the IT to write a short program to simplify end-of-day reconciliation and had the BLOM branches remaining open for a full extra hour, up to 1:30 pm, while employees were still able to leave at 2 pm. The extra hour of customer service gave BLOM a nice competitive advantage and my team a "winner aura" after in its first three months of existence.

As your team multiplies the winning initiatives, the winning spirit becomes a great morale booster and can become quite addictive, which is a good thing. Unfortunately, a by-product of that can be excessive self-confidence and cocky attitude. This you have to combat:

112

The first thing I was taught when becoming a father was that when you reprimand your child, you should always use: "you did x, y and z wrong" and not "you are bad or you can't concentrate or where is your head?" The point is, your child is reprimanded for what he did, not what he is. The same, in opposite, applies to building a winning attitude in your team, so you should say: "We are great because we did x, y and z" and not, "we are great because of who we are". You should make sure that you don't have in your team a sense of entitlement.

Entitlement, as in "I am great because I belong to this race or this religion or this country", is possibly the biggest plague facing this world. Many more wars have been fought because of race, religion or nationalism than because of ideology and vision. You want a sense of belonging and team pride obviously, but you don't want that positive emotion to turn into a sense of entitlement, where your team feels superior to others simply because it is your team. To combat that, you must keep the team constantly striving for accomplishments and you must recognize accomplishments made by other teams. You must emphasize action, not existence.

A related concept is being generous with effort. I often hear people complaining: "I am not paid enough for what I do. For what they are paying me, I should work less." or "After this new restructuring, I was given new responsibilities, but I wasn't compensated for those responsibilities so I may want to refuse them." That's the type of attitude I don't understand, and don't encourage: what is the pleasure in being at work the same amount of time but working less? What is the pleasure in having a lower level job when you can be functioning at a higher level? For me, being able to accomplish more is more important than being paid more. In addition, instead trying to get a bigger slice of a cake, I strive to work on increasing the size of the cake, so my slice is automatically bigger.

There are organizations that need to be prodded before they will increase your compensation, but for the large majority of organizations, your compensation will track the value you bring through your work. So, use your energy to deliver more value, not to argue over how to divide the bounty.

2. Encourage transparency and credibility:

Bill is a fictional character who has managed to have all the traits of an average bureaucrat with little upside potential. How much do you have in common with him?

- Bill's mother is a great cook, but refuses to share any of her recipes. When Bill himself asked for some of the recipes because he was going to live on his own, she gave them to him with slight variances, thereby ensuring that he can never replicate fully her cooking work. Bill has great technical skills that he acquired over the years as a manager, but he is reluctant to teach them all to his subordinates. When I asked him why he was so stingy on training his staff, he replied candidly: "If I teach them everything I know, they will get promoted and possibly replace me. I have to keep something that distinguishes me from others."

- When Bill is asked for his input about a particular project or product, he usually gives a noncommittal response and waits for others to shape the debate. He will then support the consensus if he agrees with it, or remain silent if he disagrees. When I asked him why he was so unwilling to commit to an opinion, he answered: "Anything can go wrong in any project. I don't want to get the shaft if a particular project I like faltered."

- In the same context of plausible deniability, Bill always try to have all his subordinates endorse in writing all of the major decisions he makes. That way, he is never on the hook for anything and his subordinates cannot trick him into making a mistake.

- Bill treats any information as a treasure, to be used sparingly and only when needed. He encourages every person in the office to confide in him or provide gossip about someone else, but he only reciprocates if it can further his personal agenda. He will rarely tell you anything that you don't know, but he will exchange information with you if it is the only way to get information out of you.

- Bill hates all his bosses with a vengeance and believes them all to be both incompetent and lucky. However, you would never know that from the way he treats them: totally deferential, pleasant, ready to accommodate, the ultimate yes man. However, he only implements the parts of their requests that he agrees with, using passive resistance to fight their other requests. He has panoply of valid excuses (system issues, staff not qualified, other competing initiatives, interdepartmental rivalries, etc.) to justify why he didn't get something done.

- Bill likes his staff to be average and discourages winners. He rarely has great performers working for him, and when that happens, he usually

114

finds a way to discredit them and get them reassigned somewhere else.

- Bill always takes the credit for whatever his unit accomplishes, even if he had nothing to do with it.

- Bill doesn't like any change and will resist it, for fear he might lose some power as a result of it.

Whether we like it or not, there is a part of Bill in each one of us. To succeed, we need to "kill Bill" (pardon the pun) both within us and within our team. We need to adopt the following principles:

- No matter how old we are, we have the opportunity to grow and become better. If we don't grow, we are doomed to failure or mediocrity and we cannot grow if we keep doing the same things and if our subordinates don't grow. There is opportunity for talent everywhere in the organization and the success of your subordinates reflects on your managerial skills. Therefore, you should not see threats where there are none and should teach and train your subordinates to be able to replace you, because if you're irreplaceable, you cannot grow.

- It is our duty to contribute our experience and knowledge to the benefit of the organization. Withholding pertinent information or opinion about the viability of a new project or product, or, worse, giving wrong information in order to be politically correct constitute despicable behavior which is bound to be uncovered at some point.

- Good leaders are not afraid to take responsibility for decisions that they make. Top management understands that anyone can make a mistake, which is why they respect people who acknowledge their mistakes.

- The information you obtain in the course of your work is not your property, but the property of your organization. You are duty-bound to share this information with others if it can help them make better decisions. Gossip that has no relevance to the conduct of the business should be discouraged.

- Your bosses are not your enemy. They are your partners in the success of the organization and want you to succeed; because that's the only way they can succeed. If you disagree with them, you should let them know and explain why. Otherwise, they will lose trust in your integrity and you will never have a chance to grow.

- Your staff has been entrusted to you. You are responsible for their growth and it is your duty to help them achieve their potential. If you sabotage them, and your conscience can live with that, you are bound to develop a bad reputation that can dramatically shorten your career.

- Stealing the credit for a good accomplishment is no different from stealing money: you are taking something that is not yours.

- Change that is good for the organization creates major opportunities for personal development and growth for the people who help make it happen.

Part of establishing a successful team culture is to "kill Bill" (thank you Quentin Tarantino!). This means you have to become a preacher as well as a leader. I personally react strongly against any "Bill-type" behavior in order to discourage it radically.

Apologies to all readers named Bill for creating this fictional character.

3. Foster humility and compassion:

There is a difference between being a good performer and being an elitist. The good performer is interested in achieving good results on a consistent basis; the elitist believes he is bound to perform well because of who he is. The elitist has contracted the entitlement virus and can be detrimental to your team: unless you are running a very focused and specialized team, you are bound to have employees from all walks of life, with varying levels of achievement potential. All your employees must feel they are part of the team, not just the best ones. This doesn't mean that you should never fire or sanction your underperformers, just that you need to create a nurturing, respectful culture that encourages everyone to do her best.

There are a number of ways to foster humility and compassion. While your personal style differs from mine, I am happy to report that the following work as far as I am concerned:

- I thank everyone whenever they give me anything, whether a report, a memo, some good news, a glass of water (at the restaurant), etc.

- I make sure I greet everyone I know, whether on the street, at a reception or anywhere else.

- I usually have an open door policy. I sometimes refuse to listen to an employee grievance because he is trying to go over his boss's head, but I always know both sides of the issue if I am refusing to listen to it.

- I don't make people wait to see me, unless there is a very valid reason why they should wait.

- I don't overindulge with outward signs of wealth.

- With everyone, I genuinely listen before I talk. If I feel that my counterpart is anxious to get his message across, I will repeat my understanding of his message before responding to it.

Most importantly, I never make the mistake of believing that old is bad:

- Many managers who take over a new division or who acquire a new subsidiary tend to treat the taken-over team almost as prisoners of war: many employees get fired or encouraged to resign, many others find themselves reporting to someone less qualified, but coming from the right place. As a result, turnover goes up, productivity goes down and company performance goes down.

- Likewise, many managers, when confronted with a new situation, can only get comfortable if their own team takes over all the reins. This is sure to create a climate of passive resistance, which will impede the desired result.

- I make it a point whenever I step into a new situation to adopt and be adopted by the existing team. When we purchased a bank in Egypt and I was placed as a CEO for the initial phase, I took over the secretary of a managing director who had to resign as part of the management transfer. As I saw in her great potential, I immediately got her involved in major initiatives. She was invaluable to me both in performance and in sending a message to all the staff and customers that there would never be an "old versus new" culture in the bank.

CHANGE MANAGEMENT

A culture such as the one described above should meet little resistance. Most changes, however, give rise to employee and manager resistance: those who feel threatened by the changes will fight them, those who stand to gain will support them... and quite a few will piggy-back on the change process to implement some hidden personal agenda. Let's call the change-resisters "enemies', the change-supporters "friends" and the opportunists "opportunists".

If you're making change happen, you should quickly understand who among your team is playing each of the three roles and respond accordingly:

- I typically will give enemies the benefit of the doubt, at first. I will explain the changes, focusing on what they perceive to be threats. I will discuss the threats and show how they can be converted into opportunities and I will assure them that I will be supportive of them throughout the process. I will make some adjustments to the new environment to suit some of their concerns if I feel they are legitimate. Beyond that, I will make it clear that the change is happening, whether they support it or not. If they continue to resist, I will make sure to confront them head on.

- I will definitely support friends and show my appreciation. I will reward them for believing in the new vision and helping in making it happen.

- I will keep a close eye on opportunists, as they can be treacherous. I might give them some concessions to win support, if I feel these concessions are reasonable. Otherwise, I will deal with them as enemies, using reason and support at first, confrontation later.

In any environment you are trying to change, you should have these three categories of people. If the friends outnumber the enemies, you have done a good job planning and communicating the change. If the enemies are too many and too vehement, you may have miscalculated and need to delve deeper into their concerns: what you are trying to implement could actually be bad for the organization.

I make it a rule: I don't try to win all battles, I don't marry my first idea and I use resistance intensity as a gauge of the soundness of my idea. After all, the team also usually has the best interest of the business in mind, so it may have seen some problem I didn't.

****

The Best Decision I Ever Made

Bassam was in his early fifties and was an office clerk in the cards operation section of the Retail Banking Division of BLOM Bank in Beirut. He had been with the bank for many years, so his salary was more than double what office clerks usually earned at the bank. He was usually the first one to arrive, around 6:30 am, though work officially starts at 8 am. He also stayed late, leaving around 6:30 pm when other employees usually left at 5:30 pm. However, he was physically heavy so he was reluctant to accomplish certain tasks such as ferrying mail between the main head office and the Retail Banking head office, a task that required a 15-minute walk each way. Plus he had a liver problem that sometimes made him fall asleep at his desk for a few minutes every day. Otherwise, he was very motivated and extremely pleasant, with a great sense of humor. Though he was widely liked, many people in Retail Banking who were much younger found it awkward to give him orders. To them, he was like an older uncle, and they couldn't see themselves telling him to take a paper here and photocopy a file there. Being slightly mischievous, he would notice their awkwardness and tease them about their own work, all in good fun. His boss, Lami'a, had no such problem and would handle him very rigorously, which was very funny to see.

Bassam had been with Retail Banking for about 10 years, when Jocelyne, my deputy at the time, came to me with an interesting offer from the Human Resource Department: Our investment bank, BLOMINVEST, needed an additional office clerk, and Human Resources were considering Bassam for the position. It looked like a win-win situation: the work at BLOMINVEST was much less hectic in terms of number of transactions and files, so Bassam would be able to fully fulfill their requirements, we would get a younger and less expensive office clerk and Bassam would have a less stressful environment. I immediately agreed and announced the news to Bassam, who approved the change, noting that the main head office was a more convenient location for him in terms of his daily commute.

The following week, Bassam was transferred to the Human Resource Department, pending his reallocation to BLOMINVEST, and we welcomed Bassam's replacement, a highly motivated young man who became productive very quickly.

A few days later, Bassam came to see me: he had not been transferred to BLOMINVEST as promised, but had become an SOS office clerk, and would now be sent to different branches when their office clerk was absent. That job was only 9am-2pm, so he would lose much of the income he earned from working overtime. I inquired and was told that the Human Resource Department management had changed their minds about sending Bassam to BLOMINVEST after a final review of BLOMINVEST's requirements.

At any rate, Bassam was not pleased: he needed the income to take care of his sick mother and wanted to be reinstated back to Retail Banking. I had given him my word that he would go to BLOMINVEST, so I told him I would do everything in my power to reinstate him. I sent a note to the Human Resource Department asking for Bassam back, and they quickly complied.

I then had to explain internally why I was bringing Bassam back, especially that his replacement had been doing a great job and was greatly disappointed to have to be sent back to the SOS position. I told my concerned staff that I was totally in favor of removing underperformers who had done a poor job, especially after they had been given a chance to improve; something that I had done several times before. This, however, was not Bassam's case since his performance, while not stellar, had been satisfactory. I said, for each one of us, there is probably someone out there who can do the job better and for less money. We are not in the business of replacing our staff every time someone better comes along; we are a team, a family, and our team spirit and loyalty are assets we want to cultivate.

At any rate, Bassam was elated. In his ten years with us, I had never seen him happier. He was happy the whole day, every day.

About three months later, Bassam took a public van to go from Beirut to Tripoli on his day off. During the trip, a speeding car smashed into the van from behind and threw it into a ravine. Bassam died on the spot.

****

120

Chapter 5: Team Growth

In my almost 6 years at Booz & Company, I recall having attended 5 training seminars: Introduction to consulting, the writing course, the presentation course, the job management seminar and the WHEEL, a new approach that Booz began to use to structure its work. Some of these seminars lasted only one day; the longest I recall was 4 days. Assuming 230 working days a year, and accounting for travel, I probably spent about 2% of my time in formal training in my Booz days. By contrast, many corporations take pride in the number of training hours they provide to their employees, often budgeting 8-10% of employee time in training. I am willing to bet, however, that none of these companies is able to come close to Booz in terms of employees learning. The reason: Booz has structured its work so you learn continuously on the job. Every report you produce there is the result of a collaborative effort from the entire team, led by an experienced principal and/or partner, discussed much like the case studies at Harvard Business School. Every assignment is structured with the participation of the entire team and the guidance of the senior members of the team. There is a vast library of the firm's "intellectual capital" called "Knowlege-on-line" which is available to all employees. I once downloaded the entire library of the firm on credit cards prior to starting a credit card assignment and found out that, after spending two days reading, I knew more about the subject than professionals who had years of experience! After leaving Booz, I used to joke that I had an MBA from Columbia and a "Turbo-MBA" from Booz.

The very strong process skills acquired at Booz and the extent of on-the-job training I have had there have biased my approach to personal growth: in my post-Booz years, I was known to be very stingy in terms of sending my teams to courses and seminars, preferring the on-the-job approach and encouraging everyone to read. I was also very careful in allowing trainers from outside the bank to come and do seminars or training sessions at the bank. The reason: every trainer uses a certain approach and will teach that approach, which sometimes may conflict with the bank's culture, or with the culture you are trying to build. For example, a trainer might teach your staff to offer the same service to all market segments when you have determined that you want different services and prices for different segments. Or to sell all products with equal intensity when you want as an institution to focus on 3-4 key products. Another worry is that the outside trainer may learn the key strategy of the bank, and then incorporate it into his training for other banks, which means he is spreading your competitive advantage around. At one point in my career, I used to insist on vetting all training sessions conducted inside the bank by an outsider.

Most executives, however, don't have a strong background in management consulting or a very clear idea of the culture they need in place for their team. It is therefore important for them to get support in the form of outside training or consulting to renew their ideas and add to their portfolio of management tools. Another positive point of making time for outside training is that it takes you away from your daily routine and forces you to reflect outside your environment; that alone can make it worthwhile. With my Booz experience fading away, I became a stronger adept of outside training.

While a fan of short training courses, I take a skeptical view of employee quests for higher diplomas. In my mind, there is such a thing as too many diplomas, and I know many employers share my views: Top management consulting firms, for example, hire few if any Ph.D.s. This was explained to me once by a McKinsey recruiter: "We may hire a few Ph.D.s for research, but definitely not for our core consulting practices: we view them as too theoretical." For a career in business, a good MBA is more than enough, and by no means essential. I have occasionally had an employee neglect a promising career track to take time off for an MBA, and I have made it clear to him that I view it as a mistake. I believe you should consider an MBA only if one of these two conditions are met:

- You are at a point in your career where you are being static, and would like things to pick up.

Or

- Your organization is actively encouraging you to get an MBA.

However, it should be clear that not getting higher degrees is in no way an excuse to stop reading and learning. I can honestly say that, as far as I am concerned, I have never either stopped learning or even reduced the pace of learning. At 50, I am learning as much if not more than I was at 25.

I have often pushed employees to get an MBA, not because I thought it would improve their job performance, but because it would help them improve their image vis-à-vis other members of top management, which would help me promote them.

122

Our focus in this chapter is how to get the team learning and growing. As the team leader, the biggest part of that responsibility lays on your shoulders. In keeping with my modus operandi so far, I will not dwell on the obvious part of training and teaching, and focus instead on concepts that I see missing in most team environments.

One of those concepts is teaching someone to be a winner: when we think of training, we think of technical skills or managerial skills, we make sure the person we are training has the ability to win, but we rarely believe we need to build in that person the motivation to win and the winning attitude. To stress that point: a champion swimmer must know two things: how to swim and how to win. In every discipline, including management, you need technical skills and winning skills.

So how do you teach someone how to win?

- You foster a positive atmosphere around her, showing her that you believe in her and count on her. You let her run things under your close supervision but with no safety net, to demonstrate your trust in her abilities. I firmly believe, and I have seen it happen, that you can take the same person and convert her into a winner or a loser simply by exposing her to a nurturing environment as opposed to a destructive environment.

- You give her assignments of increasing degrees of complexity. You start her with simple assignments that she can win easily, and then turn on the heat gradually. You congratulate her every time she makes a win, always emphasizing the positive.

- You treat her fairly. You treat everyone fairly. You make sure the workplace is an even playground where objective criteria rule. This will increase her confidence in her ability to succeed and will make her value her success more highly.

- You show the way: you don't make hasty and rash decisions that can turn against you. You have the courage to make the difficult decisions. You study every step yet act quickly, so you exude the confidence of a winner.

- You monitor her to check for signs of self-sabotage. You delicately but firmly block these wrong moves, explaining why they will lead to problems. She probably already knows in her subconscious that these initiatives will doom her to failure, so by exposing them you are moving them to her conscious and helping her become better aligned.

- You work on her motivation to win.

And how do you motivate someone to win?

- You link his actions to an achievement.

I recently ran into an office boy in the elevator. I asked him how his day was, and he replied: "Well, it's the end of month, so I am spending my time going back and forth to the Central Bank to get the salary lists for various government entities!" My response was appreciative: "Good job. Thanks to you, 50,000 employees will have their salaries in their accounts tomorrow."

- You create a positive atmosphere in the workplace.

Your employees should not be worried about being successful. They should not feel that their success is somebody else's loss or that they have coworkers being jealous of their wins. You need to convey the message that there is room for everyone to win and advance and that each person giving great performance makes the pie larger for the entire team. You need every employee rooting for every other employee. One way of ensuring that is by making sure that each employee has a specific area to work on.

- You develop in him an interest in the content of the work.

If you work for a car company, your employees should enjoy driving a nice car, be interested in design details; be drawn to new technologies to make the car lighter or more fuel efficient. Loving content is key to increased focus and motivation.

Let me pause and elaborate a little about focus.

Peter, Paul and Mary are three executives for a turbine manufacturer flying from New York back home to Los Angeles after an interesting seminar. Peter feels tired and has no specific passion, so he spends the flight surfing channels on the seat TV. To pass the time, he drinks heavily during the flight, so arrives plastered to LA. Paul is a Sudoku champion and a movie buff. Paul watches a great movie on the flight and spends the rest of his time on a Sudoku book. Mary has really enjoyed the seminar, so she spends the entire flight reviewing the seminar material and making plans to apply some of what she learned to her job in LA. They arrive LA and all go home. The next day at work,

- Peter feels tired and has a slight hangover.

- Paul is fresh and relaxed, ready for a heavy workload.

- Mary makes a splash on arrival with new techniques to improve performance.

124

I am not a fan of one-track-minded people who have only one interest: I find them boring and often limited. I am more of a Paul than a Mary. But the point is,

- Peters of the world, people who can't seem to get interested in anything, will never be winners.

- Pauls of the world will be winners if they also feel passion for the content of their job. If not, they should look for a job they can love.

- Maries of the world will be winners. They should work, however, on developing some outside interests, as a well-rounded personality will not only make them more interesting but also contribute to their job performance by broadening their horizons.

So far, we have mainly discussed how you, as a leader, can help your team grow as executives so as to contribute more to the team. You should also keep in mind that learning is not a question of hierarchy or seniority: you, as a member of the team, should also be learning and growing, and a big part of that learning will come from people reporting to you.

It has been my experience that there is a mass of knowledge you can obtain from books or from the experience of other organizations in the same business. Beyond that, there are certain secrets of the trade that you can only get through practice, especially when you are pushing the boundaries of the field you are in.

My experience in retail banking at BLOM went through two stages:

1. In the first stage, I was building the business at BLOM using my own knowledge and analysis as well as the best practices of other leading banks worldwide. My deputy, Jocelyne Chahwan, having had experience at the Bank of Montreal, was one source of such procedural knowledge. Seminars provided by VISA and Mastercard as well as other providers, supplemented by industry newsletters such as Lafferty were also great sources of information.

2. After a few years, I realized that my team and myself had reached the limit of what we could accomplish by imitating other banks and that, to make more progress, we would have to push the boundaries of available retail banking knowledge. So we did push the boundaries, experimenting with new approaches, and carefully monitoring the results. In the process, we all learned new things that we shared. In the field of sales of retail products, Jocelyne was able to identify key success factors that were a

revelation to her and to me when she did share them with me.

Achieving excellence in any business involves applying best-known practices then entering into that exciting area where your team is a source of new discoveries in that business.

But to reach that level of growth, you need to be working on all cylinders: just as a car with one cylinder will be slower than a car with eight cylinders, so will your team if each of its members is not operating at full capacity. That's why you should encourage all your team members to be ambitious and to work toward their goals.

Sometimes, one of your team members will grow beyond your capacity to promote her. Your natural reaction may be to sabotage her career growth, to create new hurdles she needs to pass before advancing or even to set standards for her that are much higher than the standards for anyone else, including you. In doing so, you might slow her down a little, but you will have lost your credibility as a leader, which means you will have compromised your own chances to grow.

Your subordinates need to be able to trust you as a leader, which means you need to be fair, even at the cost of losing resources.

One of the cases we discussed at Columbia Business School in the early eighties involved an executive running a unit in a large corporation. He was doing well and looking forward to a great career when senior management moved to his unit a younger man with everything you could ever want in an executive. As I remember the case, the younger man was smarter, quicker, with a better handle on the business and better relations with the executive suite. In short, his worst nightmare. The case was discussed in one of those specialized pure management courses where the number of students is limited and the professor, much like a shrink, states problems but wants everyone to have his own answer. Thus, there was no correct or incorrect behavior assessment from the professor, so students were left free to state their true unfiltered reactions.

As I recall it, most of the 10 or so students in the class stated that if they were the executive in the case, they would fight for their territory by sabotaging the younger man in one way or another. It shocked me that these MBA students were displaying a complete lack of faith in their

126

ability to succeed, and I took the opposite track:

- If I am an executive doing a good job and looking forward to a promotion, then I should be more than qualified in my present position.

- Enter a young cub who, by my own assessment, is more qualified than I am to run the unit.

- If this guy is one in a million and is so great, he is likely the next CEO, so let me align myself with him and facilitate his ascent, which means we can both prosper together.

- If this guy's only ambition is to run my unit, I should approach top management and tell them I have found my replacement, so I want a more challenging position. If they have a good relation with him, they will appreciate my request.

- In any case, sabotaging the young man is the same as sabotaging myself, both in the eyes of top management and in my own, as it would brand me to myself as an unethical person.

The final concept I would like to reiterate within the team growth chapter is the importance of conflict in the growth process. We all crave a stress-free work environment, devoid of conflict and disputes, where each one pursues her goals for the greater benefit of the team. Unfortunately, this is a utopian dream and the reality is that some level of conflict is necessary to keep performance improving.

This doesn't mean you should pick random fights with all your team members. It does mean you should not avoid confronting team members who are becoming too complacent or are slipping in performance. Confrontation should not be vulgar, insulting or humiliating: it should be instructive, fair and firm.

Too much confrontation leads to a loss of focus and energy, in addition to increased frustration for the entire team. No confrontation means mediocre work. Somewhere in between is the balance between a productive and a trouble-free work environment.

****

Team Growth: Time vs. Talent

Most corporations are complex environments: in order to grow and assume more responsibilities, there is a certain amount of experience you need to accumulate and acquiring this experience means spending some time on the job.

Some of the time one usually spends before getting promoted is a function of opportunity: a new higher position may take more or less time to be vacant. Sometimes a need suddenly materializes, and other times the institution seems to be caught in a long recession.

Some portion of the time to promotion is incompressible: many positions, particularly those involving a major amount of managerial complexity, require someone who has been working long enough to have seen all kinds of situations that could be encountered.

The remaining portion of the time to promotion is a factor of the concerned employee's talent.

When I joined Booz, there were five main levels:

- The Consultant level, where your end-point is business school.
- The Associate level, the entry level for MBAs.
- The Senior Associate level, where one is expected to manage small teams.
- The Principal level, where one is expected to manage large teams, be a key interface with the client and bring new business to the Firm.
- The Partner level, where one is expected to take ultimate responsibility for assignments and develop a platform that generates business for the Firm.

Booz employees would jokingly refer to these levels as "the finders, the minders and the grinders". The term "finders" referred to the principals and partners, bringing the business, while "minders" referred to senior associates and principals managing the execution and "grinders" referred to associates and lower-level consultants doing the actual work.

128

If you started as an associate, you would be expected to move to the next level, senior associate, within 2 to 3 years or be fired – "counseled out". You would be promoted within 2 years if you had stellar performance and/or were lucky enough to find yourself needed for a job management position and 3 years if you had normal performance and/or no job management position is immediately available. It likewise takes 2 to 3 additional years to make principal and 3 to 4 extra years to accede to partnership.

I found the same trade-off between time and talent at BLOM, where I started the retail banking business in 1998. Since that time, it has been growing annually at a rate of around 40%, creating a need for a new infrastructure and management positions in fields that existing bank employees were not familiar with. In addition, other areas of the bank were also witnessing sizeable growth rates, which meant that talented middle-managers were needed in their own areas of expertise. Also of note, we had a very specific culture and were pioneers in the field of Retail Banking in Lebanon, so raiding other banks for talent was not an option either. The only solution, therefore, was to grow managerial ranks from within at a pace that was far faster than the usual career progression standards of the bank. However, to ensure that the proper talent was in place to fill the role, we had to select the fast-track employee from within a pool of up to 50 trainees or other employees.

Four years before the start of retail banking, BLOM's Head of Human Resources, Dr. Pierre Abou Ezze, had the foresight to see a need for young managers in all areas of the bank and created a fast-track program geared for branch managers that was later adapted for other areas. Dr. Abou Ezze also instituted a program of standard tests at key promotion levels to ensure that the selection criteria contained objective elements. These tests were instrumental, in my opinion, in ensuring that key positions were filled with well-rounded managers able to cope with new environments and technologies.

****

Chapter 6: Team Follow Up

So, you have the dream team, well organized, well-led, well-trained and with a great culture. How do you make sure nothing goes wrong? What kind of processes do you need to put in place so your perfect team remains perfect? How do you make sure that the dream team is indeed delivering dream results?

Ask these 3 questions to any seasoned manager and she will probably reply with one word: "Control". She would be right, but the devil is in the details: Control is, as we will see, a double-edged sword.

Cool, spiffy sentences tend to make their mark on me. Early in my Booz career, a highly driven senior associate who was my project manager gave me some strong advice: "Elias, always remember that trust is good, but control is better." I had heard that phrase somewhere before, so I knew he had not invented it, but I disagreed with it intuitively, since my experience was that heavy control can kill motivation. I later learned that the phrase is said to have come originally from Vladimir Lenin.

My father was very dedicated, honest and loving, but he was also a control freak, so I learned from an early age that (a) control can be demotivating and (b) most control processes can be evaded. Other than being a control freak, my father was very caring, emotional and nurturing, and disagreeing with him was so painful for me emotionally that my mind always worked overtime in trying to find a convincing rationale for why I was right. This applied whether I informed him of my disagreement or not, and mostly I kept the disagreement to myself, so the exercise was more for me than for him. I therefore do owe my father a lot for helping me develop my critical mind, and certainly what became one of my favorite mottos: Control is good, trust is better!

Trusting another person does not necessarily mean forming an emotional bond with her. It means trusting your own ability to predict how she will behave under certain circumstances. This is achieved by knowing that person and observing her in a variety of situations. I like my close team to be composed of people with whom I share the same values and principles, so I know that I am safe relying on them.

That, however, doesn't mean I don't keep tabs on them, or that I accept whatever they tell me blindly: Even the best can make mistakes, be given wrong information or mishandle an issue. Even the best are at the mercy of self-sabotage or lack of know-how and they are often too proud to request your help. That's why surrounding yourself with people you trust, while more important than control, does not waive the control requirement. But controlling has to be handled subtly and with finesse.

Most people do not like to be micromanaged, but that doesn't mean they want to be left completely alone. As a boss, you are also a coach and a sounding board. You need to spend some time listening, you need to keep track of initiatives, ask why deadlines are not met and sometimes even step in and take over if you are sure that a deadline will not be met.

Personally, I am impatient (in a very nice, enthusiastic and positive way) and I don't like to delve into details. But I try to keep my impatience in check with someone who reports to me so I make sure that she tells me the whole story and that we are following her tempo, not mine. If she's on the right track, I will not ask for details and I will let her handle whatever she is doing her own way. If I feel she is lost or going the wrong direction, I will ask for more and more details until I am satisfied that I have found the source of the problem.

My employees have a free hand, as long as they are achieving the desired results. However, I immediately step in when they stop performing. In many cases, they know much more than I do about what they are doing, but my involvement forces them to reevaluate and reconsider, and often they are the ones who find the corrective action.

None of us knows it all, so we often have someone reporting to us knowing much more about her subject than we do. That's no excuse for not taking responsibility when she is in trouble. I have seen many supervisors admonish their employees about getting better results, without ever specifying how. And for good reason: they don't know! That just frustrates the employee and makes her look for another job. Yelling unspecifically will never get you anywhere. You have to step in, even if you have no idea how to solve the problem and take ownership: brainstorm; get outside resources, experiment, whatever... The point is, take ownership: it will yield better results.

Anticipation is a great control tool. When you are with a subordinate and asking questions, you should estimate his possible answers in your head before he replies. If his reply comes close to your estimate, he is probably progressing according to plan and you have nothing to worry about. If not, he has hit turbulence and you need to understand why. So if he is to submit a proposal in five days, you estimate that he should have the market research results already, in order to have time to analyze them. You ask: "So how is the market research looking?" If the answer is "I don't have the results, we have had a snafu, but we're working on it", you know you need to involve yourself in the process. In my experience, "we're working on it" is a sure sign that the boss needs to get involved.

You will have succeeded as a boss if your employees view your involvement as a help to them. You will have failed if your controls are so intrusive that your employees resent them and you. Controlling without imposing is an art that all managers - and parents - should learn to master.

One fatal mistake that I see many managers often doing is playing "power games" with people reporting to them. Take the example of Harry, the CEO of a large printing company that we will call XYZ. The company's marketing VP, a high-flying executive, recommended two of his best performers for a seminar on a new printing technique not used, and not scheduled to be used at XYZ. The VP wanted the seminar anyway because she believes her team should have a complete view of what is going on in the market, so they can better position and pitch XYZ. The Head of HR agreed and signed off on the training, but the CEO vetoed it under the pretext of cutting down on expenses. But XYZ was at the time very profitable, and the seminar was not costly. Harry had made the decision hastily and was not really convinced, but felt that retracting it would be a loss of face for him. In reality, the loss of face was for the marketing VP and the Head of HR who both felt unable to make the smallest decision.

Insensitive managers such as Harry typically experience high employee turnover in their organizations and are usually only left with those who can't find another job. Not a pretty situation to be in!

I was once discussing high turnover with one of those unpopular CEOs, and he replied: "Who cares? One person leaves, that's an opportunity to

132

get a better one!" What that CEO did not see was that high turnover erases the collective memory of the company. If the top people in IT have turned over several times, it becomes impossible to remember all the reasons why we selected this system over that other system, and how we are dealing with certain quirks in the core system software! If all the top admin people leave, it becomes difficult to find out why we selected this vendor over that other and what particular issues our organization has that can only be resolved by that vendor! Not to mention documents becoming more difficult to find, company secrets getting spread all over the industry, etc. In a perfect world, everything is documented and everybody is replaceable. In the real world, there are underperformers that you want to see go, but having a high turnover in essential staff is a killer, so you need to fight it.

Fighting high turnover is essentially done by building loyalty, and loyalty is a symmetrical emotion: You cannot be loyal to someone who is not loyal to you! Getting loyalty comes from giving loyalty.

There are many ways to demonstrate loyalty to your employees:

- Be on their side in their moments of weakness, such as an illness, the death of a loved one, financial trouble.

- Be strong in your public support to them if they make a business mistake or they fail in one of their objectives (assuming you really believe in their long-term potential), but by all means make sure you privately address mistakes and their causes.

- Support them when they have a problem with a subordinate or with your own boss.

- Show faith in their initiatives.

- Build a supportive, enjoyable work atmosphere.

- Give specific and exclusive responsibilities: not the same assignment to two people with blurred lines of responsibilities.

In encouraging people to remain with you, you must also look at financial considerations. In the BLOM Bank culture, which I find very successful, there is a strong reliance on incentives to bring people to competitive pay packages. As I am writing these lines, my fixed salary represents only 40% of my total compensation, with the remaining 60% coming from an administrative bonus (about 20%) and a quarterly incentive scheme based on business volumes and profitability. My deputy, Jocelyne, has a similar compensation structure. Other leading institutions I have had the chance to observe have similar arrangements for senior executives. Such compensation structures create a feeling of partnership, which breeds motivation and loyalty. I tend to prefer simple formulas directly based on performance to stock options which tend to reflect market fluctuations.

A final part of team follow-up is providing feedback. Ideally, this should be done informally and on a continuous basis. Most organizations have a formal appraisal system to ensure that feedback is provided at least once a year. Sadly, I have seen many managers ignore even that yearly feedback session, depriving their employees of that one chance to learn how they could improve. I have seen even more managers provide wrong feedback in order to keep good relations with the employee. One time, I had a bank employee request an appointment: she was being transferred to another branch even though she was perfectly happy at her branch and had a glowing appraisal. I compared the copy of her appraisal she had provided me with the copy filed at HR and found out that the branch manager had added negative feedback after having given her the review, something which was not only unethical but also against the bank's procedures.

These gutless managers usually have a short managerial career and end up rerouted to positions where they have fewer employees. As a top manager, one of your duties is to make sure that managers under you are able to lead their teams effectively. A formal way to check on manager supervisory skills is the 360-degree appraisal. In this system, someone completely detached from his department evaluates each employee. The evaluator proceeds to interview every person connected with the employee, be it his bosses, his employees or his peers, then prepares a write-up that summarizes all the findings. This system has the dual advantage of including feedback from other than supervisors and of providing an unbiased view. It is used at top consulting firms such as Booz&Co., but I do not recommend it in less complex organizations because it takes too much time and resources. What I do recommend is to keep informal channels open with people at all levels of the organization in order to spot cases of poor management. For my part, while taking care not to undermine my direct reports, I keep my door and my ears open to everyone. I don't always like everything my managers are doing, but I respect that each person may have a different management style and interfere only when truly necessary.

134

****

A New Paradigm to Improve Executive Performance

Your nephew, who you haven't seen in five years, suddenly shows up for a month-long vacation at your house. Mathew is thirteen and has a very high admiration for you, even though he doesn't know you very well. You have been very close to his father, your brother, and are keen to leave a good impression with both the father and the son. Trouble is, the boy is a tennis aficionado, and has decided that you can coach him into making the team at his school. Your tennis knowledge, however, does not go much beyond watching the US Open Finals on TV.

Fortunately, you have many friends at your local club and have been able to find Mathew quite a few training buddies. Only, he expects you to watch him in play and to provide coaching.

Your first thought is to elicit feedback from Mathew's training buddy, but what you get is not substantial enough to provide Mathew clear direction.

You think about the problem and come up with the following conclusion: I have a player I can observe plus I have access to the feedback of quite a few training buddies of his; what I am missing is a structure for orienting that feedback in a format that Mathew can adapt into a set of training objectives.

That's when you think of a three-sided approach for evaluating Mathew: succeeding at tennis, you decide, requires mastery of three different dimensions:

1. Physical strength, fitness and stamina, in order to keep a high level of performance in long matches and to impact strength to the ball
2. Mental strength, fitness and stamina, in order to keep the concentration and the hunger for winning, especially in high pressure important matches
3. Technical tennis skills, such as hitting a flawless backhand, having a good second serve or anticipating the ball

Rudimentary as it is, this framework enables you to add value to Mathew's tennis performance by focusing on the areas that need work:

- Does he seem tired after less than an hour of play? Does he have a good style but little punch? You enroll him in a gym to increase strength and endurance.

- Does his performance level decrease during matches? Does he seem intimidated by his opponents? You spend hours with him working on his motivation and his stress levels.
- Does he mishit a lot? Does he miss many balls at the net? You hire a tennis instructor to work on his style and focus on specific techniques.

This physical/mental/technical framework can be useful in any sports and in most disciplines, including in how to improve your performance as an executive. In my experience, however, an even better paradigm to enhance executive performance has the following three dimensions:

- Transactions
- Systems
- Vision

WHAT IS THE TRANSACTIONAL DIMENSION?

A transaction is a unit of work that comes to you: If you're a call center attendant, every call is a transaction; if you're a loan officer, every loan is a transaction; if you're a doctor, every patient is a transaction and if you're an airline pilot, every flight is a transaction.

It is hard to believe that you can be successful at your job without being successful at transactions since, more often than not, transactions define your job. It is therefore self-evident that you need to master transactions in order to succeed at your job. So,

- If you're a call center attendant, you should learn your products and develop a pleasant, yet quick customer interaction.
- If you're a loan officer, you should learn the intricacies of credit analysis.
- If you're a doctor, you should keep up-to-date through seminars and readings.
- If you're an airline pilot, you need to log in enough flying time on enough different planes.

So far, so good; I have just stated the obvious: To succeed at your job, you need to learn your job.

136

Time for an original insight: Our education is biased in favor of perceiving that mastering the transactional aspects of the job is all that is required to succeed in life. How come?

Consider that, from the time we are born until the time we graduate from college, most of us evolve in extremely structured environments and only encounter transactional challenges: everything is organized for us, and we just have to learn and respond to tests. Even extracurricular activities are generally well-patterned with specific roles that need filling.

Rewards and punishments throughout all our childhood and early adult life are usually all based on transactional performance: your parents are happy when you get good grades, your teacher flanks you when you write a lousy paper, your first boss gives you a good performance review if you accomplish exactly what she asks of you.

Many jobs, not just entry-level jobs, have a very high transactional content: many lawyers, doctors and engineers can reach a high level of success by being purely transactional. However, most managerial jobs require another set of skills.

WHAT IS THE SYSTEMATIC DIMENSION?

Mary is what you call a wunderkind. At her competitive school, she was always at the top of her class. Her positive demeanor and her high energy made her extremely popular and she has always had more friends than she could handle. At the Ivy-League college she attended, she was admired by both her professors and her fellow students, and would often win the "most likely to succeed" awards. Her first boss called her "the dream subordinate", impressed as he was with her high dedication, her ability to learn and her capacity to solve problems. She earned promotion after promotion until she became the youngest executive to take charge of a business unit. As business unit head, she had do deal with a very complex environment and to work very long hours. Like her, her direct reports had to stay at work very late and come to work most weekends, and top management was pleased to see the energy expended by the whole team.

Unfortunately for Mary, her main competitor across town, Walter, managing the same line of business for another company, was gaining market share. Coincidentally, Walter was appointed to head that business line at his company the same week Mary had been given her promotion. At that moment in time, Mary had a 50% market share of the business to Walter's 25%. Within a year, Walter had reached 33% share and Mary had gone down to 45%. In addition, Walter's profit margins had increased while Mary's had decreased. Nothing in Walter's background or behavior had portended these spectacular results: Walter was always in the upper middle of his class at his public school and state college, he wasn't his CEO's first pick to head the unit and wasn't particularly admired by peers or subordinates. After he assumed leadership of the unit, Walter kept his regular working hours, which were strictly nine-to-five, on account of the golf game at six that had become part of his daily routine. Walter's weekends were sacred: he had to spend time with his wife and two lovely boys to compensate for his evening golf absences, so he made it a rule to forget about business for the entire weekend.

I knew both Mary and Walter socially, and found it interesting to see how Mary was attributing her market share loss to the unpredictability of the market while Walter was boasting that his superior management skills enabled him to penetrate the market better. Since this was a very stable business with no revolutionary product introduced by either side, I decided to probe further to understand Walter's success, and I talked to customers and distributors of both Mary and Walter's products. This is what I found out:

Mary, it turned out, was a transactional manager, outstanding at being able to solve problems as they occur, but limited in her capacity to identify potential problems before they occur. Because problems in this line of business can be many, and because Mary is very hard-driven, Mary ended up spending most of her time putting down fires and doing most of the work herself.

Walter, by contrast, was a systematic manager, gifted at setting up work procedures and controls designed to make sure everyone in his team is functioning according to expectations. In contrast to Mary, Walter spent most of his time observing his team and intervening only to rescue a subordinate from making a mistake or to coach him into attaining better results.

The Walter vs. Mary story is a great example of the systematic dimension: Both Walter and Mary need to be strong transactionally, in order to react to problems, answer questions and understand their business. However, being good transactionally is not good enough to succeed in a complex organization: One must, in addition, have a systematic, organized mind in order to be able to keep the business safely flowing and achieving.

Being both transactional and systematic is a great step toward executive success, but there is one additional dimension that one needs to master in order to achieve greatness.

Harry is a solid CEO: he rose through the ranks for thirty years before reaching his current position, and knows every nook and cranny in the organization. He is a great transactional manager: very fast decision-maker, very smooth with both customers and employees, a great communicator and very well-versed in even the smallest details. He is also blessed with being a great systematic manager: he delegates just the right amount, has the right controls in place to alert him to any potential problems and is able to keep surprises to a minimum. Observers who know Harry can only find three faults with him:

-   Being on top of his business, he can spot major changes in customer patterns very early as they start affecting his sales and margins, but he is never able to anticipate them. He is therefore always a follower and never a trendsetter.
-   Every time a small mistake happens, he goes crazy trying to see what procedure allowed it to happen and revising procedures to ensure even the rarest errors are detected. This often results in added bureaucracy, slow operations and poor customer service.
-   Because he wants to make sure he doesn't miss a trend, his product portfolio is very complex, difficult to learn and expensive to maintain.

Harry's missing gene is the visionary gene. A visionary manager is someone who can set trends, sees "the forest for the trees" and has a clear focus. She typically would have a wide range of interests beyond her field of business; a good listener, although she doesn't have much patience for small talk and a reluctance to get bogged down in details. She is very comfortable in making decisions, sometimes even decisions that others might find risky. She has a strong sense of purpose and likes to keep things simple.

The visionary dimension is the top of the pyramid. If you're not transactional or not systematic, you will likely never reach a position in the organization where your visionary skills can be utilized. You may become a thinker, a professor, possibly even a consultant, but you will not get very high in the management ranks.

You may also spend years growing before you are able to utilize your visionary skills: if the organization you are managing is small or relatively simple, you may not really need those skills. However, as you grow in your job and as your area becomes more sophisticated, you will definitely need them.

139

Non-visionary managers begin to show signs of strain as they get promoted to positions of high complexity. A non-visionary manager, out of his depth, will generally be recognizable by the following:

- Always trying to catch up
- Tries to be all things to all people
- Has made up too many rules and systems
- Becomes indecisive
- Area of management reaches capacity, stops growing

BOOSTING PERFORMANCE IN THE THREE DIMENSIONS

Having identified the three dimensions, the idea is to improve performance in the dimension among the three that is the weakest. This is not impossible:

- Most of us, in our careers, evolve naturally from transactional to systematic to visionary. In the IT industry, many future leaders started as programmers or engineers dealing with single problems before they acquired the skills to become effective CEOs. A case in point is the legendary former CEO of Intel, Andrew Grove, who started as an engineer.
- At least one of us, Steve Jobs, started out by being a visionary and acquired systematic skills later on in life: After founding Apple, he had to cede the CEO position to a more seasoned manager, John Sculley, in 1985. By 1996, Jobs, who had earlier been called erratic and temperamental, had returned to run Apple, a company on the brink of failure. His systematic skills must have improved tremendously since he was able to save Apple and run it very tightly from that date onward.
- Michael Dell seems to have grown from systematic to visionary. He manifested his systematic skills very early on in life: as a young boy selling subscriptions to the Houston Post, he noticed that the two segments most likely to respond were newlyweds and new dwellers. He then targeted these two segments by creating a database from county records of marriages and mortgage applications, earning more than many of his teachers. As he grew up and founded Dell, he reached a point in 2004 where he felt a new vision needed to take shape, and he stepped down as CEO in favor of a seasoned strategic

140

consultant named Kevin B. Rollins who had earlier been a high-flyer at Bain & Company. After a while, Michael Dell must have felt he had become stronger on the Visionary dimension, and his Board of Directors must have concurred, since he came back as CEO, replacing Kevin B. Rollins.

If you have identified which dimension is your area of relative weakness, what remains is for you to implement a self-improvement program focusing on that area:

How to strengthen your transactional dimension
Your weakness in the transactional dimension could be stemming from a lack of knowledge/experience in the functional aspects of your job, such as writing, IT, legal or product knowledge or from a weakness in interpersonal skills such as public speaking, networking, handling employees, etc. In both cases, there is a variety of learning media to help you improve: books, seminars, courses, special coaching.

How to strengthen your systematic dimension
The first step in improving your systematic skills is being aware of your need to improve them. This awareness should result in your reexamination of your work habits with a view to make them become more systematic. A systematic colleague or boss could provide valuable feedback: - What tasks are you doing that could be delegated? - What types of problems are you encountering in your daily work? Are any of them repetitive? If yes, how could they be detected and avoided? - If you were to suddenly go on a long vacation, what problems would arise? Why? What processes do you need to put in place so your long vacation becomes a nonevent?

How to strengthen your visionary dimension

To paraphrase the typical management consultant, becoming a visionary requires you to "think outside the box". This means gaining access to new perspectives. In the short term, you will improve your visionary dimension with the following actions:

- Getting out of your routine through seminars, even if not directly related to your discipline.
- Networking lunches or dinners with customers and competitors, listening to their feedback.
- Reading about your industry or your function

In the longer term, you need to train your mind to become inquisitive by broadening your interests:

- Developing new hobbies that improve your mind
- Reading about all kinds of subjects, especially business success stories
- Meeting interesting people from outside your function or industry and learning about their challenges and success stories.

****

CUSTOMER YOU

144

Introduction: Your Customer and You

A customer is usually someone who purchases products and services provided by you or by your team. Given that definition, your customer can be internal or external: an external customer is outside the boundaries of your organization; for example, if your organization is the Coca Cola Corporation, a normal consumer is an external customer and a supermarket that sells Coca Cola product is also an external customer. However, if you are in charge of human resources at Coca Cola, you mainly have internal customers to consider: your bosses are your internal customers, as are the company employees and other areas of Coca Cola that rely on you for their hiring, training, compensation and other Human Resource needs.

I am not going to make any distinction between external and internal customers: in my opinion, both should be treated with the utmost respect and the skills required for dealing with either are the same. It is those skills that I seek to help you improve.

The purpose of this section, then, is to improve your interpersonal skills including selling, negotiating and presenting. It is divided into 6 chapters:

The first two chapters deal with customer needs and wants:

Chapter one discusses what the customer wants: it shows you how to listen to the customer, then makes the case that you should sometimes ignore what the customer wants!

Chapter two focuses on selling: how to convert a latent desire into a strong customer need.

The next two chapters deal with customer energy:

Chapter three defines customer energy and shows you how to use it to your advantage.

Chapter four tackles the subject of negotiation, which is what happens when you are going against customer energy.

The final two chapters deal with realizing your agenda:

Chapter five shows you how to shape your personal agenda in a way that ensures its success.

Chapter six helps you deal with the multiple agendas that we are nowadays encountering in most organizations: consultants, auditors, regulators, etc.

Chapter 1: What the Customer Wants

In whatever business or organization, there are two ways to fail:

1. The first is by not listening to your customer
2. The second is by listening to your customer

Of course this statement is caricatured and meant to catch your attention, but if you understand it fully, it might save your professional life. We will begin with the first part, which advocates listening to your customer, and we'll call it

LISTEN TO YOUR CUSTOMER!

You're probably aware of the need for anyone to listen to his customers and getting ready for some boring rehash of industry literature on the need to put the customer first. Rather than waste both of our times in this expected rehash, let me instead ask a simple question: If 99.9% know how important it is to listen to their customers, why are so many people and organizations not listening to their customers?

A friend of mine, Kay, was recently complaining to me about her CEO's contempt for customers. Kay was the Head of Private Banking for a small bank located in Europe, reporting directly to the CEO. When a few of her big customers requested to see the CEO, she naturally assumed that the latter would comply. She went to Gary, her CEO, to schedule the meetings, and was shocked by the exchange that took place:

-"Why do they want to see me?"

-"I guess they want to see who is running the show, maybe negotiate some of the rates we are giving them."

-"It's your job to negotiate rates"

-"But what they want is beyond my authority"

-"Tell them rates are not negotiable"

-"I have, but coming from you, they might accept it better"

-"It's not my job to see customers!"

-"I understand, but these are big, very profitable customers. If you don't see them, they'll perceive it as a slight and could close their accounts."

-"No one will blackmail me, customer or no customer. The bank is bigger than anyone."

About two years after this conversation, Gary was fired from his CEO position due to underperformance. He was replaced by a much humbler, customer-friendly person.

Gary's ego trip is typical of many managers who revolt against customer rule. In the typical organization, employees are taught that the customer is king. An entry-level employee has many masters: his various bosses plus the customers. In addition, he is the lowest on the totem pole. As he grows, the employee gradually has fewer and fewer bosses and more and more subordinates until he reaches the ultimate he can achieve. At that point, he has no or very few internal bosses, but he is still supposed to treat his customer as a king. Many people have egos that grow together with their career growth and can't accept the fact that they are still the customer's servants.

This ego problem manifests itself even more aggressively when the customer is an internal customer: anyone who has ever worked in a large organization can tell you stories about managers in administration or HR or IT who forget that other business units are their customers and treat them with condescension. It's been my experience, however, that the top people in support areas become more humble and internal-customer-oriented as they grow within the organization.

The point is that as we grow, our ego grows too. We need to constantly remind ourselves that our purpose is to serve and that we can never become more important than our customers. You can be successful without being humble, but if you want to reach your maximum potential, you will need a certain dose of humility.

Ego trip is not the only reason why organizations would ignore their customer wishes; for many entities, it is ignorance or disorganization. Or it could be conflict between external and internal customers.

Lebanon is a country with Christian and Moslem citizens. There, people

148

of the same religion tend to live in the same neighborhood. In 2008, a Kuwaiti supermarket chain called TSC decided to expand into Lebanon. Its first step in this expansion was to purchase the existing supermarket leader, a French franchise called Monoprix. One of Monoprix's flagship stores was located in an upscale section of Beirut called Achrafieh. The residents of Achrafieh are typically Christian, wealthy, French-educated and very European in their lifestyle. Their favorite shopping place was the Monoprix located in their area, so they were weary of a Kuwaiti chain taking its place.

My wife, Janine, was an Achrafieh-Monoprix shopper, even though we lived in a more mixed neighborhood. Initially, Janine was delighted with TSC's management of the supermarket: the French products were maintained, but a range of US imports were added, so the choice given to consumers became wider and Janine and I predicted great success for TSC. A few months later, however, other changes began to take place and I saw Janine charge into the living room very upset:

-"What's going on, Janine, what's wrong?"

-"The TSC in Achrafieh has been completely changed!"

-"What do you mean?"

-"Remember the big area where they used to sell all kinds of wines and alcohol?"

-"Of course I do"

-"Well, Elias, they have relegated this area to the back of the store and secluded it with its own cashier, as if it were a separate store!"

-"Maybe, as a Kuwaiti company, they don't know many suppliers of alcohol, so they sold the right to sell alcohol to someone else."

-"That's not what it looks like. In fact, it feels as if they were ashamed to sell alcohol and as if we should be ashamed of buying it! Plus, they have reduced the varieties of ham they offer, so I am suspecting this has something to do with religion."

This made sense to me: TSC's shareholders were Kuwaiti, and both alcohol and pork were prohibited in Kuwait, which is one of the strictest Islamic countries. One or more of TSC's shareholders must have impressed on the management the need to be very discrete on selling products which are deemed unacceptable in Islam. I continued my conversation with Janine:

-"So, what did you do?"

-"I complained to the manager in charge."

-"What did he say?"

-"There were many other customers complaints. He told us all that he would relay our complaints to the top management."

A few weeks later, TSC became a cause celebre in the Christian areas of Beirut: many people received SMS messages urging them to boycott TSC because of its attempts to "Islamize" Lebanon; there was a Facebook group founded for the purpose of encouraging a TSC boycott; customers took to filling their shopping carts to the rim, then leaving the supermarket without checking them out. Even political parties got involved in the battle and the TSC shareholders in Kuwait began to receive calls from key Lebanon political figures.

After a short while, TSC finally relented: it went back to selling alcohol and pork products without any restriction. In addition, it started inviting customers, via SMS, to "cheese and wine" tastings that included, in addition to the cheese and the wine, selected fine hams and other pork-based delicacies. This public-relations campaign was quite successful, and the supermarkets started to get more and more business.

If you needed an illustration of why you should listen to your customer, the TSC story would be ideal. The story also provides a good example of an internal customer, namely the shareholders, with an agenda other than long-term profitability.

DON'T LISTEN TO YOUR CUSTOMER!

It probably wasn't very hard to convince you that listening to the customer was a good thing: I did not exactly invent the concept which has been around for centuries! On the other hand, you are probably dying to know how I can at the same time advocate that you not listen to your customer.

Blindly listening to the customer makes three assumptions:

1. The customer knows what he wants
2. You play no role in shaping what the customer wants

150

3. The customer views you as a commodity supplier, not as a partner

As you will see from the next two examples, these are very dangerous assumptions to make.

The latter part of the 1990s as well as the first part of the 2000s saw the rise in sales of Sports Utility Vehicles, better known as SUVs. Many people replaced their cars with SUVs, which were viewed as larger, safer and more fashionable. Prestige carmaker BMW introduced its first SUV in the year 2000; by 2002, it had already become its third best-selling model, after the 3-series and the 5-series.

Besides being sexy, convenient and safe, SUVs were also heavy and gas guzzling. In the USA, the shift from cars to SUV was bad for overall fuel efficiency. Carmakers began to dodge federal fuel efficiency standards by classifying SUVs as trucks rather than cars, meaning that they were officially making more efficient fleets of both cars and trucks, even though gas consumption was dramatically increasing!

American car makers were not only happily jumping on the SUV bandwagon, they were taking great pains to create ever larger and bulkier SUVs such as the Hummer, the Ford Expedition and the Cadillac Escalade, just to name a few. When reminded that they were contributing to global warming, pollution and inflation, they would invariably invoke their duty to offer products that the customer wanted. In the mid-2000s, I read an article in the Wall Street Journal quoting a car dealer as saying something to the effect of: "Customers value fuel-efficiency about as much as cup holders when selecting a new car to purchase". It didn't sound right to the Wall Street Journal reporter or to me then, and later events began to demonstrate the fallacy of US car maker strategy: Gas prices began to go up dramatically, while consumers' incomes did not increase. As a result, demand for cars went tragically down, more so for gas-guzzlers than for regular cars. Of the three largest US carmakers, two – General Motors and Chrysler – went bankrupt.

You might be tempted to believe the classical "we did nothing wrong, we were the victims of an economic downturn" litany of most executives at these carmakers. In fact, they did cater to consumer tastes, which at that time favored SUVs. Is it their fault if the consumers later changed their minds and became frugal?

The answer is a resounding YES! And for more than one reason:

- Consumer tastes are to a large extent the result of advertising and media influences. If you had been touting SUVs in all kind of commercials, and had been paying filmmakers to display large SUVs driven by up market housewives played by charismatic actresses to make your products more glamorous, you cannot complain that you are just following consumer demand. You have been shaping consumer demand and taking it in a direction that you should have known to be unsustainable.
- Consumers tend to place a large amount of trust in large corporations: they trust that the car they buy will function properly and will not put their lives at risk, they trust that the carmaker will honor the warranty and fix the car for free during the warranty period, they trust that the specifications provided by the manufacturer as far as gas consumption and horsepower are correct, etc. To a certain extent, then, consumers trust that carmakers have their long-term interest at heart and would not propose cars that would harm them in the future.

So what would I have done if I were a carmaker? Certainly offer SUVs if everybody else was offering SUVs, but also:

- Prepare for the future by working on hybrid and alternative energy cars. Toyota had a hit with its hybrid Prius.
- Emphasize small and medium size SUVs that are more energy-efficient. That's what almost all non-US carmakers have done.
- In corporate communications and media, emphasize issues such as environmental responsibility, educate the consumer, emphasize cute and sexy over bulky and powerful. Even in the golden years of the SUV, small cars such as the Volkswagen Beetle and the BMW Mini experienced huge success.

Summing up my point, let me refer to Verena Kloos, the president of BMW's DesignworkUSA, as quoted by Businessweek on June 15, 2009: "The trick is to show consumers what the next big thing is, not reflect what they think now."

For a more dramatic illustration of the pitfalls of "listening to your

152

customer", look at the financial crisis of 2008. In a nutshell, the crisis, which caused losses to investors in the trillions of US Dollars and the losses of millions of jobs, was caused by the overextension of housing loans to "subprime borrowers". Subprime borrowers are people who have low credit scores and are considered to be at high risk of default. I have explained, in an earlier chapter, why banks would want to make such loans, so the part that interests us now is why borrowers would apply for them.

In other words, if you knew that your income was barely adequate to cover your current expenses, why would you go and take a big loan to finance a house you cannot afford? The answer is again: Consumers tend to place a large amount of trust in large corporations. So this is probably going on in your mind as you get baited by the "fast approval" mortgage peddled by your banker:

Ok, I know I can't afford it, but my banker knows that as well. These guys spend millions on financial models to study credit risk, and the people who devise such programs receive millions in bonuses and live the great life in their Hampton homes. So, according to them, somehow, I can afford to buy this great house and if I can survive the financial stress, I'll probably make a lot of money on the price appreciation in a few years. Should I be a loser and let the opportunity pass me by or grab the chance to make some money? Hey, if my banker is ready to take the risk on me, why shouldn't I?

Turns out your banker will later blame you for taking a mortgage you knew you couldn't afford!

So, when "listening to your customer", make sure you follow two rules:

1. The customer's desires are not inflexible and independent of you: the customer expects you to interact with him and educate him about your product or service, because, to him, you are the specialist
2. The customer trusts you and considers you to be his safety valve. Even if he requests something from you, he expects you to tell him if his request is unreasonable.

If you are part of an organization, your bosses are also your customers. The above rules also apply -especially apply- in dealing with your boss.

The majority of businesspeople I have met in my career try to guess what their boss wants then provide it to her. This is a wrong approach. The correct approach is to forecast what the boss SHOULD want and sell it to her. You are closer to your job than your boss is; it is therefore your duty to explain your point of view before implementing your boss's decision.

****

Put Time on Your Side

Time can be your friend or your enemy, depending on what position you take. The good news: it is not too difficult to know where time stands on any issue.

Technology, for example, is a friend of time: the more time goes by, the more things get automated and computerized. So, purchasing a typewriter in 1980 would have been going against time.

When I first started at BLOM Bank and was working with a small group of driven achievers on what sometimes seemed like a colossal task of restructuring branch operations and introducing a new culture, I often told my team: Everything we are doing is something that the bank will eventually do; our value-added is only that we are getting the bank to do it sooner and faster than if we had not been involved. Sometimes, we have used this argument to convince a manager or an employee afraid of change.

Putting time on your side is like sailing with the wind in your back: it makes life that much easier and gives you a high moral ground to stand on.

If you read the newspapers and have a moderate business culture, it should be easy to identify the direction of time:

In politics: More freedom of expression, more accountability (therefore more bureaucracy and regulation), more transparency, more freedom of movement across countries, more trade, etc.

In business: More globalization, more accountability (therefore more bureaucracy and regulation), more transparency, more technology, more innovation, more scale advantages, etc.

Whether in your personal life, your executive life or your children's education, you should be aware of global long-term trends and make sure your plans are in harmony with them.

****

Chapter 2: Selling

If you are in a general management position, you are probably spending at least 25% of your time selling: to your customers, to your team, to your boss, to your shareholders, to your regulators, etc.   There is always someone you have to convince of something!

As you are reading this, you probably have in mind the usual stereotype of the good salesman: gregarious, affable, bon vivant, very social, loud and always the center of attention. In my experience, these are the qualities of salesmen of "commodity" products, products with simple content where the room for maneuver is limited. Increasingly, however, products and services are becoming complex, so the selling process is also an educational process, where the customer learns from you how what you are offering fits his needs. For that kind of selling, a whole new paradigm is required.

I happen to be someone who is not ideal for commodity product sales, but very gifted in complex selling: In my career as a private banker selling mostly time deposits and managed accounts, I can honestly describe my performance as average. While I am great at being courteous, giving a trustworthy image and giving good service, I don't drink (bad liver), I hate smoking, I sleep around 10 pm, and I prefer the company of one or two good friends to being in large gatherings.   In addition, my casual conversation tends to be more analytical than the norm, so I am not the perfect companion for "just hanging out". Within the boundaries of institutions, however, I excel at marketing complex projects or ideas. Just before I left Booz, I saw a table with the classification of partners and principals according to total amount of sold assignments for the year. Out of about 15, I was third on the list, with the top seller being the head of the region (he is automatically credited for any work sold in the region) and the number two someone with whom I worked on establishing the initial relationship for his top customer. Not bad for a first year principal!

After leaving Booz, I went to BLOM Bank where I was able to sell management on major change in branch operations as well as on entering and conquering the retail banking market, quite a feat given how conservative the Bank is. In my more than fifteen years at BLOM, not a week has gone by without my having to make 1-2 major sales pitches to internal and external customers.

I am not boasting merely for the sake of boasting. I am boasting to reassure you, the reader, that there is a strong practical basis for what is about to follow: a model for the successful sales pitch. I developed the model with my experience in mind, so it is based on relationship selling. However, as you will see, it applies extremely well to retail and mass-market sales.

The model has identified four sales pitch categories, which are, in order of effectiveness:

-   The order ("Must")
-   The demonstration ("See")
-   The story ("Fun")
-   The suggestion ("Could")

The Must-See-Fun-Could model posits two points:

1. Any sales pitch you are likely to make falls into one of the four Must-See-Fun-Could categories or is a cross between categories
2. Everything else being equal, your sales pitch will be the most likely to succeed if it is in the Must category, then the See, then the Fun, and the least likely to succeed in the Could category

Let's explore the categories:

MUST

We have seen in the YOU section of this book how choice was a source of stress. It is also a source of work: As a buyer, if I have a choice between two alternatives, it means I have at least 4 things to do: (1) Study alternative 1, (2) Study alternative 2, (3) Study if I really need any of the 2 alternatives and (4) Study whether a combination of the two alternatives could be the best way forward.

So if you come to a customer with a product or idea which leaves her with many unanswered questions or many ways to proceed forward, she will

158

likely postpone the decision, probably for a long time. If you manage to structure your presentation in a way that leaves her no choice but to implement your idea or purchase your product, you have won the sales pitch.

The MUST presentation is typically structured as follows:

1. The threat: As in "you may be doing something illegal now" or "you are open to a number of lawsuits" or "you are overpaying" or "your main competitor is making new aggressive moves and your market share is in jeopardy" or "you are currently taking huge risks which are not fully understood".

2. The solution: As in "you need to make sure all your software is fully licensed" or "you need to track how your sales teams are pitching this investment product" or "it would be a great shame if you don't reduce your paper costs by using email to perform these tasks" or "you need to urgently add this popular product to your portfolio" or "you must close this risk by implementing this new monitoring system".

3. The identification of alternatives and their dismissal: As in "you have three ways to do this, but way number 1 does not fully resolve the problem and way number 2 is too complicated to implement in addition to being very expensive, so way number 3 is really your only solution".

I believe a big part of my success comes from using the MUST approach. Most people I have met usually structure their pitches to include the first two parts of MUST: they correctly identify the threat and the solution, but leave it to their customer to identify alternatives to their recommended solution. As a result, they do not get any kind of fast approval of their recommendation because the customer needs to do research before agreeing to their proposal. They fail to realize that the more you understand your customer's situation and the more you do work on behalf of the customer, the higher the chance of winning your pitch.

My first interview with Blom Bank in 1995 is a great example of a MUST sales pitch. I was tired of being an expatriate in Southeast Asia and wanted to explore opportunities in Lebanon and the USA. I was vacationing in Lebanon and mentioned the subject to my mother, who offered to introduce me to a friend, Dr. Naaman Azhari, the then Chairman of Blom Bank, the largest bank in Lebanon. I accepted her offer and she fixed an appointment for me with Dr. Azhari at his office.

Dr. Azhari had no idea about who I was and why I had come to see him; as he told me later, he thought this was the son of a good friend who wanted some kind of favor, so he was not relishing the prospect of meeting me. Despite his low expectations, he was very courteous and asked me what I was doing for a living. I quickly described to him my career and education history and he was very impressed. By now, he had understood that I might be looking for a job offer, so he asked me: "How could your background be of help to us?"

What I answered was a perfect example of the MUST sales pitch. For ease of reference, I am hereby presenting it to my readers in a MUST format:

1. The Threat: "Well, Dr., I have noticed that your branches, as well as those of Lebanese banks in general, are still organized using an old British system called the cashier system. This means that a customer who needs to withdraw cash must first go to a counter clerk to initiate the transaction, get a voucher, and then go to another employee called the cashier to give him the voucher and take his money. This means that your customers are spending too much time waiting for service at your branches. Plus, it means that your branches are inefficient, and therefore overstaffed. And I am sure that the rest of your branch processes is similarly inefficient."

2. The Solution: "I have worked on similar situations several times before. I can build a small team of BLOM employees and restructure your branch operations using the more modern teller system, which will help you reduce costs and dramatically improve service. This is something you and your competitors will have to do at some point in the future; the only reason you are still structured in such an archaic way is because the country stood still for the 15 years of the Lebanese civil war."

3. The identification of alternatives and their dismissal: "This is not an exercise you can do easily using the bank's internal resources: there will be a lot of resistance, and I am not sure you have a person who has enough experience in this that he could push it through your culture. You can also hire outside consultants to do it, but it would cost you a fortune and I am not sure the Lebanese market has these kinds of consultants available."

A very sharp man, Dr. Azhari was drawn to the opportunity and probably

160

impressed that I had come to the meeting with him having anticipated the whole conversation and being very prepared. Most people go to meetings with a "let's see what happens" approach. Successful executives anticipate what is likely to happen during a meeting and prepare accordingly. Successful salespeople put themselves into the minds of their customers and see things from a customer perspective.

I have probably convinced you of the power of MUST in small meetings. It is also used by large corporations to carve exclusive niches in mass markets:

- It has become a requirement for professionals in education and advertising to use Macs instead of PCs. It has become a must for teenagers to have an I-Phone. "Cool" people increasingly have to have an I-Pad. The Apple Corporation is bent on making exciting products and billing them as a must for the young/"in" crowd.
- Do you know many large organizations that don't use Microsoft Office? Microsoft has succeeded in making a must out of its Office product and any IT manager opting for any other solution is probably risking his job!
- Every so many years, a toy comes out that becomes the "must" Christmas present for children. When that happens, the company that makes the product strikes gold.
- The media industry is always seeking to hit the MUST pay dirt: there are the must-see movies of Thanksgiving, Christmas and the summer and the hit-tube of the summer. Is it possible to not see the latest Batman movie and not feel like an outcast?

As great as the MUST approach is, it cannot be used on all pitches: if your standard mode of operation is to predict mayhem unless people buy your product, you will be quickly dismissed and your credibility will be shot. If you have a tendency to exaggerate, people will discount everything you say.

Being good at selling does not mean having a big mouth. It means working hard to find the proper solution that best fits the customer and being honest about it. Credibility is a salesperson's biggest asset.

If your product or idea does not fit MUST, the next great approach is SEE.

If your product or idea does not fit MUST, it must be due to one of two factors:

- It does not resolve a highly urgent customer problem, and/or
- There are alternatives to your product that cannot easily be dismissed

In either case, your customer will not make any decision regarding your sales pitch, either because there is no urgency or because he has to review the alternative solutions, so there is much work to do on his part.

That's when it is time to use SEE. SEE basically involves demonstrating the product or making it available immediately.

A while ago, I saw a demonstration for a water filter: the salesman poured a can of brown soft drink into the water filter and I saw a colorless liquid emerge on the other side. I was so flabbergasted by the ability of the filter to remove colorings that I purchased the product immediately without asking any more questions, even though (1) I had no immediate need for a water filter and (2) there might have been better brands than the one I purchased.

I purchased one of my cars after receiving an invitation from the local Jaguar dealer to test all of the Jaguar cars in his showroom. Although my budget at the time did not make room for a top-of-the line Jaguar, I couldn't pass up the invitation, so I went there and tried a brand new XJ8 and another brand new XK8. When I told the salesman these two beauties would stretch my finances, he showed me a one-year-old used Van Den Plas, which was about 30% less expensive than the XJ8, yet more luxurious. After test-driving that one, it became my car for the next few years.

In my work in consulting and banking, I have often used the concept of pilot to drive major change forward:

- In reengineering a bank's branch network, Booz's standard procedure is to start with one pilot branch, test all the changes there, make sure they are successful, show it to the bank's top

162

management, then roll out the program to other branches in the network.

- When creating a new retail banking product, my team and I often begin with a "soft launch", where the product is proposed in limited quantities for a period of time, in order to gauge market demand and resolve any quirks before moving forward with a major advertising or sales campaign. This soft launch enables us to demonstrate to the bank's top management the product potential, prior to our requesting a large budget for the campaign or any other resources.

Getting the product "out there" is very prevalent in the mass market:

- At BLOM, we have compared the success rate of credit card campaigns. Campaigns were the card is pre-approved and all the customer has to do is sign are dramatically more successful than campaigns where the customer is invited to apply for the card.
- Newspapers have successfully used a one-week free campaign to gain new subscribers
- It seems to me that a majority of services you can purchase through the Internet carry free trial-periods and/or money-back guarantees.

Even courtship is a form of SEE pitching: the couple interested in a serious relationship begins with a few dates where the prospective partners can get a feel for what it would be like to be permanently attached to the other person before making a commitment.

The concept behind SEE is one where you offer the customer his time in exchange for his decision: the fact that the customer can sample the product erases all uncertainty as to the product viability. So, you have saved the customer the time and expense of determining whether the product is viable. In exchange, you ask from him to forego the additional step of looking for a similar product that could be better or cheaper, and make the decision now.

Another variation of SEE is one where the supplier compensates the customer for his time in exchange for his decision:

- Timeshare vendors will often offer tourists a free ticket to a tour or a local attraction if they agree to attend a two-hour meeting on

the virtues of timeshare. I once attended such a meeting in Hawaii and was the only attendee who did not end up purchasing.
- A very successful investment broker told me he usually invites high net worth individuals in groups of 10-20 to a prestigious hotel to conduct investment-themed presentations after which he peddles the investment services of his firm.
- Sales are a form of time-subsidizing SEE: you agree to visit a department store in a specific period; in return, you get discounts on your purchases.

SEE is not only useful if MUST is impractical: it is also used together with MUST in order to build credibility. Your MUST pitch may be spot on, but you may be someone unknown to the customer, so SEE is a great way for you to establish credentials: references are a form of SEE, CVs are a form of SEE.

Between MUST and SEE, you should be well equipped to make a quick sale. There will be times, however, when you are not in a hurry to make a sale; rather, you would like to plant the seeds of a future sale. For those times, FUN is your preferred weapon.

FUN

I called this part FUN even though it is really more about story than about fun. Why? For one, if you're like the vast majority of people, you would rather listen to a story than to a lecture, which is why you used to prefer any movie to a philosophy class, so a story is usually fun, at least in relative terms. Also, I believe that fun sells, so adding some to your sales pitch should help you in most cases.

In his book, A Whole New Mind, best selling author Dan Pink provides extensive research showing that stories are both easier to understand and more likely to be remembered than facts. In all humility, I would like to add my confirmation, based on personal experience and observation.

At Booz, and likely most other major consulting firms, reports are based on a "storyline", which is the story you tell the customer. If a newly hired consultant states a fact, the reaction from his more seasoned Booz colleagues will be "so what?" Facts have no value unless linked to a

164

cause, and stories are a collection of facts and causes leading to conclusions.

The investment world is one where stories are always present to enliven facts: your broker will not tell you that the market has gone down yesterday. She will tell you instead that redemptions from mutual funds were not matched by new investments from retail investors, leading the market to lose a few points. Or that a rumor about Steve Jobs's health put some pressure on Apple, which in turn made the market more bearish. Point is, these kinds of stories are the reason why you like to call her every day for information that you could read in the newspaper.

These stories are also why you would buy. For example, your broker might pitch: you know, there is this small metal bearings company in Kansas. Some big players are quietly amassing positions in it because it is family-controlled and the CEO is very old, ready to retire. When he does, chances are his children and nephews will sell their shares in one block and a large institutional shareholder will take it private. There is not much downside, but the upside could be significant.

Let me demonstrate the impact of FUN to you in a small, but fun exercise:

Imagine you are in Manhattan, looking to purchase a one-bedroom apartment on the Upper East Side.

The first apartment you see is on East 76th Street. It is priced within your budget, built recently, very pleasant and quiet. Its owner is a doctor who had to move to Wisconsin and the real estate agent representing him is very professional and courteous: she shows you every room and closet and responds patiently to all your questions.

The next apartment you see is on East 75th Street. It is in the same price range as the previous one, also built recently, very pleasant and quiet. This time, the real estate agent, while also professional and courteous, is slightly more loquacious: she tells you that the apartment owner is a charming advertising executive of 32 named Alice who had been living in the apartment for the last three years, after graduating from Columbia

Business School and finding a job on Madison Avenue. She met the man of her dreams two years ago and their romance led to a wedding at Saint Patrick's Cathedral and a reception at the Pierre Hotel. Because the groom is also a successful executive, they are moving to a three-bedroom coop within the same neighborhood, as they need the extra space so the family can expand. Alice, you learn, has spent a few years in Hong Kong after graduating from college, so dabbles in feng shui, which can only be good news for you if you decide to purchase the apartment. Because Alice is a busy executive, she had a cleaning lady, coincidentally named Alicia, who came and cleaned twice a week. Unfortunately, Alicia will not be available for you because Alice wants her to take charge of her new apartment that requires 3 days a week since it is bigger.

Now answer honestly: which of the two apartments would you purchase?

Having successfully demonstrated, I hope, the power of FUN, let me move on to the final, and least effective weapon in your sales pitch arsenal.

COULD

COULD is the standard recommendation pitch: you should be doing this because of that, where the argumentation does not rise to the MUST level.

If you're like 90% of the people I have seen in action, you are only using COULD in all your sales pitches. If that is the case, each one of your pitches that you are able to upgrade to a MUST, SEE or FUN will dramatically increase your sales performance.

I consider COULD to be the least effective yet most widely practiced technique, but that doesn't mean I don't use it. Because the other techniques require much more preparation, I use this in situations where I don't need immediate results and I don't have enough face time to use FUN.

To give you greater respect for COULD, allow me to digress and use biology to explain a concept I have found to be very important for the

166

sales process:

First, let me explain the egg fertilization process as I understand it: Out of the millions of sperm present in the semen, less than 1000 reach the Fallopian tubes, one of which contains an egg. Of those 1000 or so sperm, many surround the egg in the Fallopian tube in order to penetrate it. However, the egg has an outer membrane designed to protect it from invaders. No worry: the head of each sperm releases enzymes that weaken the membrane. On its own, one sperm will not be able to weaken the membrane so much as to allow it to penetrate. However, after enough sperm have released enzymes, the membrane does weaken and allow one lucky sperm to penetrate. At that point, the egg depolarizes and dumps repellent into the space surrounding it, pushing the other sperm away.

The convincing process is, to my mind, very much like the egg fertilization process: your customer's mind has an invisible outer shell that protects her against unwanted ideas and suggestions. Each suggestion, even when rejected, acts to weaken the outer shell against similar suggestions; so, the more exposed your customer is to your suggestions, the higher the chance of one suggestion being accepted.

That is why there is a place in your repertoire for suggestions that you suspect will not be accepted now, but help you plant the seeds for later acceptance.

In the world of mass market selling, I would classify media ads as a COULD tool: they suggest, which may or not lead you to buy, but will anyway plant the idea in your mind.

A final word of caution: in order to sell, you need access. You need your customer to give you enough time and attention to enable you to make the pitch. You need to establish a relationship with your customer, to answer her phone when you call. It is therefore of major importance to always maintain credibility and keep the customer interested. It means not overdoing the suggesting, not boring the customer with problems and complaints and maintaining a positive and friendly atmosphere at all times.

With both my internal and external customers, I use the concept of the silver bullet. I have a limited amount of such bullets, so must use them wisely. That means not asking too many favors, making too many suggestions or too many demands. In the field of retail banking and consumer marketing, I am an advocate of not pitching too many products at the same time and offering instead a complete but simple product portfolio.

Remember, customer attention is limited.

****

Meeting Mr. Quiz

Probably one of the top perks I have been given in my job at BLOM Bank is having Jocelyne Chahwan as a deputy. Jocelyne is a very gifted individual and has done a lot to make my life easier. However, she does have a mischievous streak and will sometimes practice a little torture on me when she sees I am too serene.

On one such day, she shows up at my door with a gentleman and introduces him with great fanfare. Since he had no appointment, I figured he must be very important, especially as she ordered coffee for him in a manner that led me to believe this interruption was likely going to last quite some time.

The man, who we will call Michael, proceeds to explain to me who he is, what company he works for and everything he has done in his life prior to joining that company ten years ago: 10 minutes have passed on this busy day, and I still have no clue why we are having this meeting. I look at Jocelyne: she is smiling ear to ear as if Michael was the best thing since sliced bread.

Having explained who he is and where he came from, Michael proceeds to explain in detail the various activities of his company. This takes another twenty minutes during which I am agonizing. Here, I must tell you that the guy is not particularly good looking and is no great orator, before I tell you that Jocelyne still has the baffling ear-to-ear smile. At this point, I have given up any hope of understanding either of why Jocelyne has introduced me to the gentleman or what I am expected to do with this introduction.

We are now way past the 30-minute mark in the conversation, when I note (to myself)that Michael has so far explained one by one 8 products his company sells, all of which could somehow be of interest to the bank. At this point, I am beginning to see some reason why we are talking, but am also surprised that he is mentioning each product as a future avenue of cooperation before moving on to the next one. That's when I make two major decisions (in my mind) that transform my mood from somehow irritated to mildly euphoric:

(1) I decide that Michael will henceforth be called Mr. Quiz, since he seems to be quizzing me as to which product I should purchase from him.

(2) I decide that I should spend the remainder of the time Mr. Quiz will be spending in my company planning in my head his

induction into my forthcoming book "Boosting YOU" as an example of how not to sell.

After the meeting finally ended, we left each other with no specific action plan going forward.

Trust me: especially with busy executives, it pays to tell the other person what you want upfront.

****

Chapter 3: Using Customer Energy

In late June 2009, I purchased an issue of Fortune Magazine with Bill Gates on the cover. The main topic covered was the best advice ever received by Bill Gates and by a number of other major business leaders. As I recall it, Bill Gates was quoting his father; others were quoting family members, colleagues, acquaintances, etc. It got me thinking about what I would answer if I was asked the same question, namely: "What is the best advice you ever received?" After a few days of reflection, one piece of advice stood as the best. With apologies to my belated father, to other members of my family, to my colleagues and friends, I must credit writer/guru Deepak Shopra for that gem. I was reading Shopra's "The Seven Spiritual Laws of Success" back in 1997 when one of the laws really struck a chord with me, namely what Shopra named the "Law of Least Effort". This law doesn't advocate leading a couch potato existence, as its name could imply; what it does is recognize that there is a certain energy in the universe and that you should try to align yourself with that energy, not try to fight it. By doing that, you will see that you are able to accomplish more with less effort.

Most people view the supplier-customer relationship as one where the supplier is exerting energy to please the customer, who is inactive. This is actually incorrect: the customer is a participant in the relationship and his energy should be used to enhance it.

The Cola wars offer a great illustration of customer energy successfully used to help the fortunes of Coke or Pepsi. Let's go back to 1975, when the Pepsi Cola Company created and publicized what it called "the Pepsi challenge". The challenge consisted in offering random consumers a blind taste test pitting one sip of Pepsi against one sip of Coke. A majority of consumers, unaware of the brands they tasted, showed a preference for Pepsi. Pepsi milked this fact to the fullest extent in its ads, creating the impression among many people that Pepsi was the best tasting Cola. Why Coke had the higher market share in the US market among the two brands became the subject of explanations: some people attributed it to Coca Cola's better marketing; in his book Buyology, Martin Lindstrom reveals that tasting a generic cola stimulates a different region of the brain than a branded cola, so consumers are affected by Coke's brand, logo, color and fragrance, not just the taste. Offering his take on the subject in his book Blink, renowned author Malcolm Gladwell explains that there is a difference between taking a sip and drinking the whole bottle or can: whereas a consumer might prefer a sweeter drink for a sip, he will choose a slightly bitterer drink for a larger consumption. Regardless of the explanation, Pepsi Cola was able to capitalize on this consumer sip preference to gain a higher profile. That's an example of a company using customer energy; read on for an even better illustration, still in the domain of the cola wars.

Fast forward to 1985 when Coca Cola, probably irritated by Pepsi's "taste superiority" which had found its way to increased market share, decided to replace its famed cola drink with a new and improved drink, appropriately named "New Coke". New Coke was sweeter, and would probably beat Pepsi in any taste challenge, enabling Coca Cola to capitalize on both the best taste and the marketing infrastructure. What happened next was stunning: although many people enjoyed the taste of New Coke, the old Coke turned out to have extremely vocal fans. According to Constance Hays in his book "The Real Thing: Truth and Power at the Coca Cola Company", over 400,000 angry letters arrived at the company, demanding the reinstatement of the old Coke. Even Fidel Castro criticized the decision to change Coke, ironically finding himself in agreement with the father of then Coca Cola CEO Roberto Goizueta who is of Cuban descent.

This customer reaction, this customer **energy** was probably the best thing that ever happened to Coca Cola: within three months, it removed New Coke and reintroduced the old formula, now named Coca Cola Classic. Customers responded, market share rebounded, and the Pepsi challenge was relegated to the confines of history!

One company I find great at using customer energy is Amazon: it has sophisticated software that uses customer previous purchases to suggest new ones, going so far as to suggest certain music CDs to customers who purchased certain kinds of books. In addition, it invites its customers to rate the products they have purchased, which increases its desirability to both existing and prospective customers. I have personally rated many products purchased through Amazon, and, as the following story will show, I am a keen user of such ratings.

I recently went into a bookstore where I was drawn to a prominently displayed novel. I took it and started looking at it: it had testimonials from major authors and was one of Oprah's books of the month. It was the first novel of an unknown author, so I purchased it, acting out of impulse. It was a long novel, about 800 pages, and not an easy read: rather than going straight to the point, the author delighted in long descriptions of mood and scenery, which is exactly what I don't like in books. After reaching page 200, I was still not captivated enough to deem the book purchase-worthy, and not bored enough to stop. I decided to go on the Amazon web site and see how the book had been rated: turns out it had a mediocre rating, contrasting with the glowing reviews printed on the cover! I usually also read the comments of readers, which I did in this case: again, many readers shared my mixed feelings about the book. After leaving the web site, I was convinced that I would not have purchased the book had I bothered to research it on Amazon first, meaning that it is not a good idea for me to make a book decision without consulting Amazon!

Using customer energy is not a concept that is valid only for retail companies or for external customers. It is valid in any customer-supplier relationship, be it external or internal.

You need to know two things about the customer energy concept, one of them positive and the other negative:

- Let's start with the good news: customer energy is not something hidden that you may have to look for; much like the thousands of angry coke letters, the stronger the energy the more it will be apparent to you.
- Now for the bad news: instead of using this energy, your tendency most of the time will be to fight it.

So what to do with the concept and how to make sure you are identifying customer energy? The easiest way is to focus on what you are fighting.

Let's use a practical example to illustrate the point: my boss is my major internal customer. All my boss's requests and demands constitute customer energy; some of them are acceptable to me and others cause me stress. I will be implementing all the requests that I find acceptable, so there is no issue there. The ones that cause me stress, I will probably resist: this resistance is a poor use of customer energy. Instead of resisting, I should try to find a way to go with it.

The CEO of one of the subsidiaries of a large group had an independent streak. Rather than implement groupwide procedures, he insisted on creating his own set of procedures which often conflicted with best practices elsewhere in the group. For example, compensation levels and practices at his subsidiary were markedly different from elsewhere in the group, without any convincing explanation for the difference. The group's top management allowed the subsidiary CEO enough leeway to create such differences with a view to giving him the benefit of the doubt ("Maybe his way is better in his market?"). After a while, however, when the subsidiary did not show major performance, the group top management became impatient and the subsidiary CEO had to resign. One person close to the action once remarked to me: "He was let go because he insisted on doing things his way. His underperformance could have been due to his unique organization or to other factors, and we will never know. If he had accepted the group's way of work, he might at least have had the group share responsibility for the underperformance!" Now, I never enter a job with a view to underperform, but the point is: accept help from your stakeholders.

In my early days at Booz, I was sent on an assignment in a Middle-Eastern country as part of a joint team involving the London office (we did not have any Middle-East office at the time). In our first day on the job, the client top executives assigned to work with us proposed that we have a daily status meeting throughout the length of the project. We immediately refused their offer, on the grounds that we would not have new things to discuss every day. Privately, we felt this would amount to micromanagement and would interfere with our independence as consultants. Reluctantly, they agreed to limit their participation to weekly meetings, which was fine with us. After a few weeks, however, we discovered that work at the client organization was extremely centralized and that there were many things we could not get done without the direct intervention of these top executives, who, as it turned out were extremely busy and extremely reluctant to make decisions except as a group. We ended up having to beg them to restore the daily meeting format, which they in turn resisted, having understood the real cost of that meeting on their own time schedule. This is a typical case of a customer offering energy and a supplier not taking advantage of it.

Another typical example of customer energy is when an internal or external customer has a problem which is unrelated to you. Your first reaction is usually to try to ignore the problem when you really should focus on it.

Say for example that you are meeting your CEO to pitch a reorganization of your area and find out that she is really only interested in a fraud that was just discovered in another department. Your reorganization is now competing with the fraud for the CEO's attention and your attempts to keep the focus on your subject will probably be in vain. You probably would be better off altogether postponing the reorganization discussion and offering her your help with her fraud case. Later, you might find an angle that connects her fraud concerns with your proposed reorganization and adjust your pitch accordingly. Or, you may not find any connecting angle, and she will be just grateful to you for being there when she was worried.

Your customer worries are often predictable: After the banking crisis of October 2008, pretty much everyone was worried about liquidity and

174

cutting expenses. That's when you should be pitching ideas that increase liquidity or cut costs. Around April, pretty much everyone worries about taxes. That's when you should be pitching tax-saving ideas. At the beginning of the year, people are usually making big plans for the New Year. That's when you should be pitching expansion and growth.

Companies in the consumer market acknowledge this point, which is why they have special "going to school sales" in September, travel deals at graduation time, promotions on diet items before the summer, etc.

One good source of worry information is auditors, risk managers and consultants. They can tell you what issues and concerns are timely in the executive suite. Of course, they will tend to emphasize issues that are important to them, so you need to be discriminating about what you take seriously.

Customer complaints and anger are a great energy source. If a customer calls you to complain, that's great news: that means he cares enough about you to educate you about why he is upset. Customers who don't care just change suppliers, those who manifest their anger should be taken seriously: they are your best potential customers. An angry customer is a customer who is giving you his full attention: once you resolve the subject of his anger, you can deepen the relationship with new products and services.

Another godsend is a customer who needs a favor: she also has to give you her full attention. The way you do the favor for her will not only earn you her gratitude, but will also showcase your effectiveness as a supplier.

Using customer energy is an essential part of your toolkit in dealing with both internal and external customers.

****

In Search of the Objectivity Frontier

A typical young person at the beginning of his career has a tendency to see things in black and white, good and evil. People are classified as great or mediocre: the former can become role models, the latter are ignored .

This bias of the young executive is normal: people at the start of their professional life have so much to absorb that they need to simplify their complex environment and they need mentors to emulate so they can develop faster.

With age, experience and maturity, however, you begin to see nuances and begin painting your environment in more than black and white:

- Your boring middle-aged neighbor who only eats certain types of foods and has weird political ideas becomes suddenly someone you might find interesting at the neighborhood barbecue because of his fresh perspective on many issues.

- You have a major disagreement with your best friend at work. You completely disagree with how he is handling some of his tasks and this affects your work. However, you discover that this doesn't make him a bad person or that you will like him less than before.

At one point, you become aware of the fact that there is wealth in every person and that no person is perfect. The good news is that this realization makes you able to enjoy richer relations at work and outside work. The bad news is that this new egalitarian vision may cause you to become indecisive and unfocused.

My friend Tom is a very smart person who has grasped very quickly the fact that people are complex. As a result, he has only friends and shies away from any confrontation. This character trait has been very beneficial to him early in his career as he was seen by his managers as wise and smooth. Unfortunately, he later on had difficulty breaking into the ranks of top management as he was seen as weak and unable to make tough decisions, especially in the field of Human Resources.

176

My first employer, Joe Audi, chairman of Interaudi Bank did me a great favor by simultaneously believing in me and supporting me while at the same time pointing to my weaknesses. This gave me early on an alternative to the black-and-white view that was in my default settings. It also demonstrated to me that you can see situations in color, yet still cut through the complexity to make fair performance evaluations and reward people appropriately.

The color view is great in dealing with customers in that it allows you to empathize with every single customer. However, as with employees, it should not keep you from providing objective advice to your customer, especially when you see a customer making a mistake or adopting a wrong strategy.

In the consulting jargon, the term "going native" is often used to describe consultants who become so close to their customers that they lose their ability to provide objective, independent advice.

A key skill to acquire is therefore operating at the "objectivity frontier", close enough to understand and empathize with the other person, without crossing into the area where you can no longer objectively judge and counsel this person.

****

Chapter 4: Negotiating

The word "negotiating" is one of those we know intuitively, but have a hard time defining. What is negotiating? A quick research on the Internet did not turn out anything satisfactory, with most definitions involving an adversarial relationship. Webster's online dictionary provided the fuzzy: "To confer with another so as to arrive at the settlement of some matter". Based on all this confusion, I see an opportunity for me to define the word. So, let's humbly make history together with my proposed definition: "Agreeing on the distribution of resources among partners".

Mexico and the USA may negotiate border control issues: who will pay for them, who will benefit, etc. You and your boss may negotiate your employment contract: how much you will be paid, what services you will have to provide, where you will be based, etc. Negotiations are usually stressful, and often adversarial as are relations among partners: whether they like it or not, Israel and the Arabs are partners in the Middle East as they share a common geography.

There are many books and courses specializing in teaching you how to become a successful negotiator. I confess that my formal education in that area is limited to one book I may have read in my late teens that abounded on the virtues of achieving a win-win negotiation (whereby no side loses). In my more than thirty years of professional experience, however, I have been involved in thousands of negotiations, so I have tried to distill this experience into a model.

I'll call my model FWET, for its four pillars:

Fairness

Work

Empathy

Transparency

Let's now talk about each of the FWET pillars:

The outcome of the negotiation should be fair for both sides. That means you give up the possibility of bullying and humiliating the other party.

There will always be times when you have such an upper hand in the negotiations that you can practically dictate your terms. If you take advantage of the situation to completely obliterate the other party, you will have achieved the following three things:

1. Short-term success
2. Deep resentment for you on the part of the other party
3. Your not feeling comfortable with yourself

The last two items are a recipe for long-term failure.

I am not advocating that you should give up any leverage you might have in a negotiation. You should push the other party to give you the concessions you need to operate at the top levels of performance, but you should stay away from being too greedy and striking an unfair deal. To determine what is fair, you should look at market prices, other similar deals and possibly the assessment of an unbiased third party. Trust me, your partner will appreciate your magnanimity and will respond in kind in the future.

Looking at this in terms of energy, a deeply unfair deal in your favor constitutes a transaction that will generate negative emotions and therefore negative energy from the other party to you as well as from your subconscious mind to you. You now have won one battle and have two new enemies.

The other side of being fair is to not give in to bullies. Throughout your career, you are sure to meet many bullies. Bullies typically only respond to threats, never to compromise. Bullies only use force and only understand force, although each force could be made up of different components. In your typical schoolyard, many a big muscular boy is successfully counter-bullied by a more socially adept, faster-talking smaller classmate. The point is, bullies believe they can scare you into giving them anything they want; you have to show them that you're not scared before they'll leave you alone. And you can use any weapon you want to show them that you can hurt them too. India's Mohandas Gandhi successfully used the force of non-violent civil disobedience to fight the forces of repression.

As a matter of principle, I do not like to give in to bullies. I would have been against appeasing Hitler and I am against negotiating with terrorists. But I am also careful not to get drawn into battles that can drain my energy. So I might give in sometimes, but I make sure not to deal with the bully again.

In defining what's fair, however, you should always bear in mind that you are a biased party: if you ask 100 persons whether they are paid what they deserve, I am willing to bet that less than 5% will acknowledge they are overpaid, when at least 20% of the people in most companies would be considered overpaid if their productivity was assessed by an objective consultant. As a rule, people tend to believe they deserve more, which means they believe they are unfairly treated. Therefore, when you are assessing what's fair, you should account for that bias and try to err on the generous side. "Be fair" in this case, means, "be generous, but don't let yourself be bullied".

Many acrimonious divorces are typical of the fairness principle going awry. The party that did not want the marriage to end exacts revenge by making excessive demands and nitpicking on small details, while the other party all too often gets drawn into futile and never-ending battles.

My advice to divorcing couples would be

- To the party that did not want the marriage to end: Don't let your rage poison the rest of your life.
- To the "guilty" party: Understand your partner's emotions. Apply the "be generous" principle. Choose your battles carefully.

WORK

Negotiating involves a lot of hard work, and the higher the stakes, the more the work involved. Some of the work takes place before the negotiation begins, and some of it during the negotiation.

180

Before the negotiation, you need to understand what's at stake:

- On your side, what are the various costs involved, how are they calculated, how are they expressed? What are the benefits you are bringing to the table and how are these benefits perceived and priced in the markets? Who are your competitors and what are the choices of the other party if he wants to bypass you?
- On the other party's side, the same kinds of questions: costs, benefits, competitors. What other choices do you have if the negotiation fails?

After you have gained a clear understanding of all the issues involved in the negotiation, you should begin to work on a number of proposals that are acceptable to you and may be accepted by the other party. For example, if you are negotiating with a talented executive a position within your company, you have a number of levers you can work with: salary, incentives, fringe benefits, sign-up bonus, geographical location, reporting lines, title, authorities, office size, etc. You should figure out what you can offer so that you can arrive with the candidate at a configuration that is right for you and exciting for her.

Doing your homework before the negotiation is absolutely essential:

- It gives you an edge as the negotiation progresses and issues need to be discussed in great depth. When that happens, the party that is the best prepared typically makes the most progress.
- It prepares you mentally for the alternative in case you are not able to reach an agreement with the other party. That readiness to walk out of the negotiation reduces your stress level as you negotiate.
- It gives you self-confidence. Being well-prepared sends a message to your unconscious that you are taking this exercise seriously.

A lot of work is also required during the negotiation: it can be very long and arduous, as issues need to be explored and clarified. Many people lose patience during negotiations, often because they assume that the other party is tricking them. In my experience, the other side frequently has a poor understanding of the issues at stake, so a patient partner who explains has a big opportunity of turning no into yes.

Many people turn the negotiation, at one point or another, into a power game where egos and personal feelings become involved. This can be due to a lack of patience: picture a tennis game where the two players are exchanging the ball back and forth. At some point, one of the players loses patience and goes for a risky smash which he, more often than not, loses. In tennis, it is called "unforced error". In negotiation, you don't have room for too many errors, so you need to work on yourself to keep your concentration and your poise for as long as necessary.

EMPATHY

A few years ago, my friend Hugh went through some difficulties in his marriage: he was almost 40, in a middle-age crisis and he felt that his wife of 10 years, Laura, was no longer the perfect companion he had married. Mind you, I only know the story from his side, so I am not going to judge who's at fault! In any case, how the marriage became rocky is irrelevant to our discussion.

During that rocky period, Hugh discussed his case with many friends and raised the possibility of a divorce. He and Laura had a lot of assets in joint name, which he was managing. He was also the breadwinner since Laura had elected to stay at home and raise their children. Many of Hugh's friends had an important piece of advice for him: move the money to your name, possibly even offshore, so Laura doesn't ruin you in case of divorce.

After mulling the idea, Hugh came up with a different approach. He went and moved a sizeable part of his portfolio from joint custody to … Laura's name. His friends thought he was an idiot, Laura thought he was a sweet man and I thought he was a genius.

I later asked him why he had done that, to which he replied: "Well, Elias, if all my friends thought of the money issues, I am sure Laura had the same concern as well. Plus, she is in a very weak position given that I am the one who brings home the bacon. I wanted to send a message to her that, whatever our marital difficulties, I would never abandon her financially."

Following this action, Hugh and Laura found a renewed trust in each

182

other and the marriage was able to survive.

Life is made up of vicious cycles and virtuous cycles. This can be found in all fields and all areas: a restaurant that sees a reduction in its business may decide to save on costs, for example by firing some waiters or being less generous with quantities or using inexpensive ingredients. The resulting lower service levels or lower food quality in turn cause more customers to stop eating there, which means the restaurant loses even more money and cannot afford to maintain even the just lowered quality standards, and so on and so forth. This is called a vicious cycle. The opposite is a virtuous cycle: the restaurant invests in new furniture and hires 5 new friendly waiters and waitresses, while simultaneously improving food quality. The resulting increase in customers brings about additional profits that are used to further improve the restaurant, which in turn attracts even more customers.

Interpersonal kindness is also subject to vicious and virtuous cycles: give somebody something for free and he will fight to reciprocate and show his appreciation; take something from him and he will become hostile.

The idea is to put the negotiation on a virtuous cycle or at least keep it from entering vicious territory. This is done by offering rather than snatching, by being generous rather than being a scrooge. Of course, there is a limit to how generous you can be; but by empathizing with the other party, you can at least know where and how to be generous.

A positive attitude is required in order to stay in virtuous cycle territory. In my career, I have encountered a lot of executives who nag constantly or make demands continuously. These people are generally long-term losers. In any business relationship, there are three parties: you, the other party to the relationship (for example, your employer, or a supplier or a customer) and the outside market. Rather than trying to extract a bigger piece of the action from the other party, you should work with the other party to gain more, together, from the outside market. Instead of focusing on getting a bigger share of an existing cake, work on making the cake larger, and your share will automatically become bigger.

Key to any negotiation is placing yourself in the mind of the other party. If you are negotiating a contract with an airline that is purchasing your planes, you should put yourself in the place of the executive negotiating the contract: Whom does he report to? How will his performance be evaluated? What are the issues he worries about? What would you be worried about if you were in his shoes? Negotiating the contract is not a game of tricking him into accepting your conditions; it is thinking together to find the clauses that will protect all of the following: the airline, its representative and your company. Anything else will fail in the longer term.

I did two distinct tours of duty as CEO of BLOM Bank Egypt. In the first one, from December 2005 to September 2006, I worked on restructuring the bank that BLOM had just acquired and putting the right team to manage it the BLOM way going forward. Since I was not interested in remaining permanently in Egypt, I had agreed with BLOM Chairman Saad Azhari that I would commute to Cairo on a weekly basis, leaving Beirut on Saturday evening and coming back on Thursday evening. The arrangement was painful since I spent 5 nights a week away from home in addition to having to work on Sundays. When, in July of 2006, we found an Egyptian CEO to replace me and he was due to start in September, I approached Saad: "Listen, the bank is running smoothly now, and I am not going to make any major changes before the new CEO takes over, so what do you think if I started to lighten my time in Egypt, say to 3 nights a week and take the morning flight rather than the evening flights?" He immediately agreed, although I did not get to execute the plan since a war broke on July 12th between Hezbollah and Israel and I was unable to fly back to Lebanon until the end of August.

Almost 3 years later, in February of 2009, we had a strategic disagreement with the Egypt CEO and he resigned. Saad wanted me to take over temporarily, and I saw the wisdom in his choice, but I couldn't see myself, at 50, resuming the grueling commuting schedule of 2006. Before I had even uttered a word, he took me aside: "Look, I really think you need to take charge of this place for now. You don't need to be doing it full time; you can spend 3 nights a week coming in the Monday morning flight and leaving Thursday. That way, you will be spending 3 nights in Egypt and 4 with your family. I think that's not too bad." I was impressed that Saad had remembered my major concern from 3 years prior and addressed it immediately as he broached the subject of my leading the Egyptian operation. This was not the first time I had seen Saad approach a problem from the point of view of the other party; in fact, he makes it a habit of summarizing points from the perspective of the other person before addressing them. This is one of his strengths and a key factor in his outstanding professional success.

Part of being empathic is responding precisely and concisely to the other party's concerns. The other party usually has no more than one or two main issues of concern. In order to be effective, you should identify these major issues and address them quickly, one at a time. Instead, many managers tend to go off subject or argue both sides of an issue.

TRANSPARENCY

There is a school of thought that assimilates negotiating to playing poker: keep your cards close to your chest, bluff, ask for more in order to settle for less, etc. In my experience, this kind of behavior does not lead to long-term success. It may get you an advantage if you are buying souvenirs in the streets of Bangkok or Tijuana, or in a contract with people you are dealing with for the first time. But if you think about it, you will find that most negotiations are done with people you will be dealing with multiple times, so trying to outsmart them will ruin your credibility.

In my experience, being honest and transparent actually yields the greatest results and builds the best long-term relationships.

Transparency means that you don't inflate your demands. If the other party does not know what market prices or practices are, you should educate him. If you don't know what market prices or practices are, you should educate yourself. Then, you should align your contract to market practice, with a logical explanation for every deviation.

Where there is no established market practice, it is often advisable to use an external, independent consultant. Accepting and quoting outside advice is a way to keep the process fair and transparent.

Transparency also means you should establish rules and boundaries that are not negotiable. In the Arab/Israeli conflicts, two fundamental boundaries have been set by the two parties: (1) The creation of an independent Palestinian state and (2) The recognition of Israel's right to exist. Establishing boundaries upfront saves time and improves credibility.

In negotiating as in every other aspect of life, people value and reward honesty and the moral high ground. The following true story illustrates the point completely:

In late 2005, our team from BLOM Bank had completed due diligence on an Egyptian bank called Misr-Romanian Bank. The latter had a large amount of bad loans in its portfolio, in addition to a large amount of contested taxes claimed by the Egyptian government for previous years. Because the final amount of losses from bad loans and lost tax litigations would only be known years later, pricing the deal was a matter of estimation. Of course, we tended to be conservative in our estimates while the selling team tended to be more aggressive, which led to a wide gap between what we were ready to offer and what the seller was willing to accept.

In an effort to bridge the gap, BLOM sent a high-level team to Cairo for three days to meet the sellers and try to find common ground. The team was composed of Dr. Naaman Azhari, Saad Azhari, at the time Vice-Chairman and champion of the prospective acquisition and yours truly. After hours of intense discussions, we asked the other side to come up with a final number, which they did. We went separately to deliberate and decided the number could work for us. Still, there was a temptation to come up with a counterproposal and a lower number. After some more deliberation, we decided to accept their number as is, so we could claim the high moral grounds. Thus, we made our final offer and went back to Beirut.

Because there were many owners involved, some of which state-owned entities, a bigger group of seller representatives had to meet to formally accept our offer and, as usual in a large group, could not accept it as presented. They came back with a higher number. That was a problem for us, especially given that our number was predicated on being able to participate in a public offering that was to take place a few days hence. Plus, their number would not work for us.

In an effort to revive the deal, Saad Azhari decided to go spend a few days in Cairo, and I went along. By this time, we were both very worried about

186

our efforts falling through as another bank had just expressed interest in the acquisition. What clinched the deal was a phone conversation between Saad and the Vice Governor of the Egyptian Central Bank, in which Saad summarized the deal from the viewpoint of the Egyptian government explaining that a deal would be much harder to reach with any bank after the public offering and that the other suitor had not performed any due diligence yet, which meant that its interest in the deal could be diluted after a close examination of the bank's loan portfolio and tax liabilities. As a cherry on the cake, Saad reminded the Vice Governor that our offer was at the exact price recommended by their own investment bankers, "we gave you what you asked for, so how could it not be the fair price?".

Within half an hour, the Vice Governor called back with the good news: our offer was accepted.

****

The Power of Simple

Perhaps the biggest casualty of our increasingly complex society is our attention span. In this era of sms and blackberries, people are constantly bombarded with short messages and this is undoubtedly taking its toll on the number of issues they are willing to explore at length. Simpler has always been better, but even more so today.

Consider this observation: A person's success is usually proportional to the simplicity and ease with which you can explain what she does. For example, the owner and CEO of the largest travel agency in Brazil is likely to have a higher impact on the world than the assistant of the head of the accounting department for the seventh largest travel agency in the province of Catamarca in Argentina.

You probably don't need me to tell you that a short memo is more likely to be read than a long one and that someone who doesn't speak a lot is more likely to be listened to when he does.

To be successful in sales and negotiation, you need to invest a large amount of effort into understanding issues, and then simplifying them. Convey a message by emphasizing major points, even if they are not in your favor, and deleting clutter and very minor issues, even if they are in your favor. Your counterparty will be grateful to you for not wasting his time.

A related concept is dividing a huge issue into smaller pieces and moving step by step toward the final goal.

Of course, if you will pardon the pun: simplifying is not simple! There is always the danger of oversimplifying and coming up with platitudes. Trust me, however, simple messages are very powerful. At Booz&Co., many partners used to pore over client presentations for hours, finding ways to reduce the number of lines in each title and making sure the messages are straightforward and easy to capture. Beneath each simple statement could be reams of data relegated to appendices or given directly to the counterpart team, but communication was simple, and therefore powerful.

A great development exercise is to study complex issues and try to simplify them: it forces you to test logical assumption and helps you find contradictions.

Clearly, however, in order to be credible as you make simple statements, you must neither be shallow nor perceived as such. This means you must work on your culture, read, be informed and be rigorous. It's a long process, but well worth the wait.

A final note about the power of simple: your product portfolio, your customer processes should ideally be simple enough that your customer can understand them and you can explain them. So a periodic exercise to simplify and even reduce the number of products and to make processes smoother and faster is a must. More is not always better!

****

189

Chapter5: Managing Your Personal Agenda

Under ideal circumstances, achieving the goals of your employer will serve your personal agenda. Unfortunately, there are many instances where this is not the case, and where achieving what your employer wants you to accomplish will go counter to your own best interests. This chapter examines such cases and the best way to deal with them.

Sam graduated from the Wharton School with a shining new MBA in the early 1990s. Unfortunately, the economy happened to be in a slowdown, especially for the financial services industry, Sam's area of preference. Because of a weak employment record prior to the MBA, Sam did not have a very strong resume, and had difficulty getting job offers. She ended up joining a newly formed boutique investment bank in which she saw an opportunity to grow with the company. She did do an outstanding job and earned lavish praises from her boss over the next three years. Unfortunately, the company did not grow to become the substantial player it had planned to be and Sam became a great performer in a small institution, something that she felt was not fulfilling enough for her. A few months later, the company CEO and major shareholder made a speech at an employee retreat in which he confessed he wanted the company to remain small, so he could control it better. For Sam, that was the signal that her future lay elsewhere.

Sam's boyfriend, Wayne, also graduated from Wharton that same year. He managed to get a job with a very large financial institution, but in the financial control area. So, instead of hopping on planes to drum up great business deals, Wayne became busy poring over financial accounts and ensuring that deals were booked correctly. Because Wayne's long-standing dream was to be a rainmaker, he figured he would apply to join the investment-banking department once the economy recovered. Unfortunately for him, he was so good at his job that his bosses were reluctant to part with him, to the point where they would sooner see him leave the company than join another department.

Their friend Eric had no problem at graduation: he joined a top management consulting firm in his favorite area of specialization and did such an outstanding job that he managed to get a fast-track promotion. After the promotion, Eric landed on a huge assignment with a key client where he also performed admirably. Only problem: the client was very comfortable with the team and would only agree to more assignments if they were staffed with the same team. That was great for the firm because it meant more billing, less so for Eric because consulting firms at the time tended to value exposure to many clients and multiple environments. Through no fault of his own, Eric was threatened with a slower career growth.

Faced with career hurdles that are independent of their job performance, Sam, Wayne and Eric all started to get their resumes out and got some interviews. Initial feedback was as follows:

- Sam was told that her resume was very weak because the company she worked for was very small.

- Wayne was told he was very specialized on the accounting side, not an ideal candidate for the business development side

- Eric was told he would probably have to take a small step back in terms of position given that he did not have the variety of experience that other consultants at his level had.

In all three cases, some permanent damage was done, proving that your career trajectory is often influenced by factors totally unrelated to your performance.

As I am writing this, I just found out that Alfred Kelly, the 51-year-old president and No.2 of American Express, who had been there 22 years, submitted his resignation. In a statement released on the 5th of October 2009, Amex Chairman and CEO Ken Chenault declared: "In the context of discussions we have had about longer-term plans for the organization, Al made clear to me that he wanted the opportunity to run a company as chief executive. Given my own plans for the coming years, we both agreed that was not likely to happen at American Express in the short-term."

My first impression after reading the statement is that Alfred Kelly's personal agenda, just like our three Wharton graduates, is in conflict with his employer's corporate agenda. Unlike the three Wharton graduates, however, Mr. Kelly seems to leave in a great position without any damage stemming from the agenda misalignment.

Mr. Kelly and the three Wharton graduates are not the only people to have experienced the agenda misalignment situation: it has happened to almost everyone I know, and it has probably happened to you several times if you've worked long enough. It is a common problem that everyone is likely to encounter at some point. It is a waste of energy at more than one level:

- Discussions with your bosses about your future take energy from you and from them.

- Stressing about your future is another loss of energy.

- Time spent networking for the purpose of finding another job is time that could be invested in your success within the organization.

If you reach a point where your personal goals diverge from the direction you are taking at work, you should apply a three-step action plan:

1.   DECIDING HOW TO REACH CONVERGENCE:

There are three possible ways you can reach alignment or convergence between your personal agenda and the corporate agenda:

1. You convince your organization to incorporate your personal agenda in its objectives: this requires open communication with your bosses, in which you are willing to listen to their views in addition to giving them your views. Discussions should be non-threatening, of the "give me your advice" kind. Very often, these discussions will lead to common ground.

2. You convince yourself to revise your own agenda: this means you take a deep breath and study, as objectively as you can, your personal agenda. Is it realistic? I have met a number of people

192

with dreams that are far greater than their capacities. Is it worthwhile? For many, the one and only career objective is making money. While money is generally correlated with achievement, there are many cases where making more money is not the best long-term use of your capabilities, which is what your objective should be. Is the divergence real? Many people overreact to a misunderstanding or to a minor incident. Before deciding there is a divergence between the organization's goals and your own, make sure that the perceived divergence is profound and structural. Getting confidential advice from one or more unbiased sources is helpful.

3. You decide that the differences are insurmountable and therefore should quickly find another employer. If you've reached that decision, you are ready for the next step.

2. KEEPING THE MOMENTUM:

Most if not all people view a person's career potential through a combination of time and position, as in:

- "My son was made Vice President at 29!"

- "After only one year, she was promoted from Assistant Branch Manager to Branch Manager"

- "Sam needed 4 years to go from associate to senior associate."

So if you have decided to make a move out of your current employer, the clock is now moving against you. This is no time to procrastinate or wait for low-probability opportunities: you should work aggressively several leads in parallel and minimize the transition period.

3. KEEPING THE CREDIBILITY:

So, you are now in your job search, aggressively networking and courting employers. Unfortunately, offers are not coming as quickly as expected and your dream job has not yet materialized. If you are like 90% of the people I have met in my career, you are likely to make at least one of these two mistakes:

Your first mistake is that, taken as you are by your job search, you will become less focused at your present job and your performance will decrease. You might decide to postpone sharing some innovative ideas in the hope that you could use them on your next job or you might feel that any great accomplishments you make would be wasted on a company you are planning on leaving. Other than being ethically wrong, this type of behavior indicates low self-esteem: it shows that you view yourself as working **for** somebody. The right attitude is that you are working for yourself even if you need an organization to give you the opportunity to fulfill your potential. Your accomplishments are part of your life and part of your CV. They belong to you and they are the reason people value you. More importantly, they are the reason you value yourself.

Your other mistake is to become impatient with the length of time the job search is taking, which causes you to jump into the next available opportunity as if it was the Holy Grail. If I look at the job offers I have received in my life, about 9 out of 10 have been less attractive than the existing job they were supposed to replace, yet I was tempted by about 50% of them! That's because novelty is sexy; the same phenomenon that applies to relationships! So make sure you're not jumping "out of the frying pan and into the fire" and study the next position carefully before you commit. It is better to remain at the same employer than change just for the sake of changing.

A related common mistake occurs when you actually commit to a new job and have to spend a transition period at your old job. Most people begin to treat their old employer as an enemy and are actually extremely uncooperative in matters pertaining to transfer of duties, training the next person, etc. Many people take with them confidential files in the hope of using them in their next role. Again, other than being unethical, these kinds of acts are ruinous to your image. Your best advocates are your previous employers; you should remain on the best of terms with them.

To sum up, there will be periods of time when your personal objectives will be different from the plans your employer has for you. To make the most out of your potential, you should strive to minimize these periods of time and strive for alignment and harmony between personal and corporate goals.

A final note on the topic: how can an employee be totally honest and transparent with his employer given that he is sometimes doing things an employer could deem disloyal, such as posting a resume with a headhunter, talking with another company about a job opportunity, etc.? My advice would be to keep these activities to the bare minimum (don't go to job interviews on a regular basis just to "price" yourself correctly) and be very discreet about them while very honest and open about anything else.

****

Do You Lose Control if You Tell the Truth?

Irina is a compulsive liar. If she goes to the supermarket, she will tell you she went to the pharmacy; if she has a hot date, she will tell you she had a family dinner and if she had sushi for lunch, she will tell you that she had a pizza. To be fair to her, she only lies if you corner her with a question; otherwise she is content living her life without providing you with any details. On work issues, Irina is careful to almost always tell the truth, because she knows she could be discovered and knows it would be detrimental to her career.

Since I could not find any motive to Irina's compulsive lying, I once asked her to explain to me why she did it. "Well, Elias", she said, "you should realize that telling people the truth about what you are doing, what you are feeling, what you are thinking, etc. means they can, with time, predict your behavior, and therefore control you. They can use what they know about you to convince you to do something they want, they can also spread rumors about you, they can use information about you to discredit you if they are competing with you on a certain subject. Knowledge is power, Elias. I have two choices: I can either tell people who ask me questions to mind their own business, which would be viewed as rude, or I could give a wrong answer. Take 3 cars, Elias: the first one you control perfectly because all its gauges are in working order, so you know when it needs gas, when it is overheating, when it is about to break the speed limit, etc. The second one has no gauges so you know not to use it unless you fit it with gauges. The third one has all the gauges, but they never tell you the truth: you may feel you have enough gas, but you're actually running on empty; you may feel you're below the speed limit when you're actually way past it; you thing you are in control, but it's actually the car that is in control! I am that third car, Elias!"

Irina is correct in her assessment that information is control, but grossly underestimating the value of being transparent. People who know how you think and have so much information about you that they feel they can predict you are also people who will trust you. A relationship based on trust is one where both parties confide in one another and lower their defenses.

196

Recent events in the Middle-East corroborate Irina's statements and limitations: with the widespread dissemination of information, dictatorial regimes are no longer able to hide secrets. With information in the hands of the people, control has also shifted to the people. However, in this age of Facebook, YouTube and Wikilieaks, it is futile for any government to try to keep control away from its people. In this age of data monitoring and internet tracking, explaining one's behavior is more appropriate than trying to hide it. Just as governments must embrace a new era of transparency and democracy, so should individual people become more transparent and truthful.

****

Chapter 6: Navigating Other People's Agendas

Howard was one of those men who believe in fairy-tale love stories that last a lifetime, in monogamy and in the notion that each one of has a soul mate. He also believed in love at first sight even though he hadn't experienced it in his high school, college or early professional years. When he met Lisa at a party around his 29th birthday, he felt as if a divine revelation had been offered to him: she was physically everything he had ever wanted in a woman and had a style that projected the image of his perfect mate. The first glance is all he needed to unleash a wealth of emotions he never suspected he could feel and he had to sit down and wait a few minutes before he recovered his voice. If he had been a doubter, that day would have made him believe in God.

The other miracle that took place that day is that, while Lisa was undeniably attractive, her charm seemed to touch Howard much more than any other men, so he did not have to fight the whole male population to date her and, miracle of miracles, she appeared to be highly attracted to him as well!

Howard and Lisa started dating immediately and began to make plans for the future. Howard had a very good job and was really keen on getting married as soon as possible, since he had no doubt Lisa was the one. Likewise, Lisa more than obliged and they started to get ready for the great day.

During that period, you could scan Howard's brain and you would find the words "happy ever after", "just the two of us", "you and I", "me and you on a deserted island", etc. He dreamt of nothing other than living the rest of his life with his beautiful bride. Howard dismissed the idea that the actual wedding preparation could drive a wedge between him and Lisa: "You think I can fight with Lisa over wedding details? That's totally impossible, and I will tell you why: because if we have any disagreement over anything involved with the wedding such as who to invite, what type of flowers, what kind of ceremony, you name it; if there is any disagreement, I will go with Lisa's opinion. As far as I am concerned, she's the boss!"

Howard's reasoning looked very sound: only two people were involved in

198

the decisions, one of whom had already committed to accept all of the other's decisions. So how could there be any stress?

Fast forward to wedding day minus 4 months: Howard and Lisa sit down and agree on everything in less than half an hour. They divide the tasks about equally and Howard gets ready to begin working on the tasks assigned to him: booking the venue, selecting the menus, contacting the printer for the invitations, contracting the music and arranging the video. Everything is looking good!

Two days later, Lisa calls him and needs to see him urgently.

They meet at his place: she wants to change almost every detail of the wedding. Turns out her father thinks the selected venue is too cheap, her mother wants quieter music, and her best friend wants to be involved the design of the invitations. And that's not all: her psychic friend does not like the hotel where they were to spend the night, and her sister had a bad dream about Cancun, so they need to find somewhere else for their honeymoon. Plus, her former college roommate is pregnant and can't travel, so there is a strong preference for the honeymoon to go through Buenos Aires where she resides. Suddenly, Howard is not feeling good: he just realized that he married Lisa... and her father, and her mother, and her sister and a couple of friends as well.

Worst of all, Howard is feeling that Lisa does not really want all these changes: she just can't bring herself to say no to all these people she loves!

If you're sympathizing with Howard's frustration, let me point out to you that it is not so different from two types of frustration we often encounter in the business world.

The first type of frustration is what I will call frustration with your leader's persona:

- Imagine that you are working at a company with many problems stemming from bureaucracy or politics. You and many others at the company believe these problems can be fixed quite easily if the CEO makes some tough decisions. Unfortunately, the CEO is tied to certain interests and shows no interest in changing the status quo. A few years go by, and a new CEO is named, someone you have known and admired for many years. You have great hopes for the company, only to find out 6 months later that the new CEO, despite all her promises, is as weak and indecisive as the previous CEO, and no change has happened in the company.

- Or, if you follow politics, remember how many officials you have voted for who had campaigned for drastic change and have never been able to accomplish their campaign promise. If you stop a person in the street, she might tell you the major problems the USA is having: lack of universal healthcare coverage, expensive insurance, abused judicial system, gun proliferation, budget deficits, trade deficits, high taxes, inconsistent foreign policy. Yet, no matter which party comes to power, these issues remain unresolved due to the proliferation of special interest groups and lobbying organizations.

The second type of frustration is frustration with your leader's real powers:

- Since our childhood, we have been trained to view the CEO as the all-powerful semi-God who runs the corporation. Recently, I saw a magazine touting "The 50 most powerful women in the World", so I checked it out to see who these women were: they were all CEOs! Every employee who feels smothered by his boss dreams of the day he will become CEO so he can run things his way.

- When he actually becomes CEO, the employee finds out that the CEO position does not really carry as much unquestioned power as generally believed: The CEO has to bow to a board, to public opinion, to regulators, to auditors (who generally report to the Board and not to the CEO), to key customers and often to key suppliers and key executives who might have leverage over the company!

I speak from experience, having seen many CEOs up-close and having played that role myself several times, when I say that a position of absolute power does not exist:

- A bank CEO has to contend with central bank regulations, stock market regulations, compliance and anti-money laundering regulations, auditors who report to the board and to regulators directly, risk management departments that are similarly autonomous as well as the press and public opinion. In addition, all major decisions are made by committees: the executive committee decides on strategic issues, the asset-liability

200

committee makes financial decisions, the purchasing committee vets purchases, the EDP committee looks at technology initiatives, etc. The CEO is often a coordinator who keeps things moving in the right direction, but can rarely impose radical views.

- Even the president of the United States has major constraints on his power: major decisions have to go through the Senate and the Congress, opinion polls, which are often influenced by advocacy groups, greatly diminish his autonomy and even his personal freedom is dictated by security considerations.

Given all these constraints, it is very tempting for leaders to do nothing or to choose the path of least resistance. As I am writing these lines, Apple, Research in Motion and Google are redrawing the mobile phone landscape to the detriment of market leader Nokia. Any armchair analyst will tell you that, in order to restore its market supremacy, Nokia must emulate the I-Phone features. As a giant company with huge resources and unparalleled experience in mobile telephony, Nokia should have no trouble copying a product that Apple, a company that had no previous mobile experience was able to develop from scratch. Why doesn't it? An example of corporate indecision? Leadership frozen by bureaucracy? If you think a little bit, isn't it shocking to see how many companies seem to have problems that the whole world except their own management appears to know how to resolve?

So, what should you do if you find yourself in a leader position, with all your potential decisions in conflict with this or that key player? Doing nothing is a waste of your time, leading you to see resigning as a better alternative.

Another way I have often seen used to ensure competing agendas are not hindering the CEO agenda is to buy all the different resistance groups with promotions, salary raises, extra staff, etc. This is one reason why many organizations have outsized overheads. This is also a trap you might fall into as you try to make major change happen.

Rather than buying people, doing nothing or resigning, you should navigate the various interest groups, negotiating with all until you reach the best solution for your organization.

This does not mean you need to water down whatever you had in mind in the first place. It means you have to make the effort needed to sell it at the various levels of the organization. You will recall from the negotiation chapter that we came up with the FWET model, where the F stands for Fairness.

In applying the principle of Fairness, we need to remember the following:

- Refraining from making a decision that will benefit the entire organization because one powerful group is against it is UNFAIR.

- Making deals of the "scratch my back and I'll scratch yours" kind as a way to run the organization is UNFAIR.

- Allowing one entity to blackmail other entities in the organization is UNFAIR.

But doing the right thing doesn't have to lead you to war with all kinds of groups within the organization. Using the other components of FWET, you can find creative ways to align the various groups toward your goals. Examples:

- Getting various adversaries in the organization to talk to each other and even to switch roles, so each group can empathize with its "enemy group".

- Changing the incentive structure (bonuses, promotions) to ensure they are aligned with your vision for the organization, not special interests.

- Appointing "champions" to lead initiatives outside their domains and following up very closely on their progress.

- Most importantly, communicating the vision constantly and stubbornly and being very transparent, if diplomatic, about things that need to change.

Even if you do all of the above, you may still face resistance from people who could be hurt by change. That's when you need to be strong and inflexible. I believe conflict costs energy for both sides, and I therefore usually strive to avoid it. However, some level of conflict is necessary for big change to happen. The French have a say "On ne fait pas d'omelettes sans casser des oeufs", meaning "You cannot make an omelet without breaking some eggs". Any change results in winners and losers, and you need to have the stomach to accept the casualties. If you are transparent about what the change entails, every person in the organization will have an opportunity to align himself with it and benefit. People who refuse it must pay the price.

To sum up, becoming a leader will not in itself give you as much power and latitude as you think. There will be hidden centers of power that will try to derail your vision because it does not suit their interests. However, this is not an excuse to keep the status quo and become a transactional manager, getting your paycheck at the end of the month and postponing change and value-adding to the next leadership.

Successful leaders of complex organizations are achievement-oriented communicators who are able to rally diverse constituents toward a limited number of goals and create positive momentum toward success.

****

Economies of Success

In my early years as a consultant, the major buzzword was "economies of scale". The theory behind economies of scale was that you should increase your size, thereby spreading your fixed costs over a bigger volume and achieving lower unit costs as a result. For example, if you hire a top-notch media consultant with her team, her costs will be prohibitive if you are a small company with limited output. But if you are a large company and she is able to increase your sales by 20%, you will more than cover her costs and overhead.

Later on, technology became more scalable, meaning that the cost of a machine and its support became proportional to its size and outsourcing became more prevalent, enabling companies to purchase as much of a service as they need. At the same time, consultants began to appreciate the challenges and complexities of size, leading them to recommend sizing up much less frequently. The new buzzword replacing economies of scale became "economies of scope". The theory in the case of economies of scope is that you can achieve economies by combining goals. For example, Amazon achieved tremendous economies of scope by expanding its offerings from books to DVDs to electronics to all kinds of other items: its costs of operating a web site and its logistics have been better utilized for a relatively minimal increase in investment.

I believe the next great buzzword applies to companies and to individuals in a similar manner. I haven't seen it used or defined, so let's make history together and identify the "economies of success".

Economies of success are a huge force in today's world and are likely to become more and more pronounced with time, as information becomes more widespread. Examples abound:

- You want to read a good book. Where is the first place you go to? The New York Times' or Amazon's best-seller list. If you see a title that has been in the number 1 spot for seventy consecutive weeks, you are very likely to purchase it.

- When you are looking to hire a new intern, you look at resumes of candidates and short-list only those with impressive college achievements or prior internships.

- In a consulting firm, Jim has become the senior partner's "blue-eyed boy" and keeps getting all the critical and juicy assignments while Eric only gets the boring stuff.

Typically, what is happening is:

- Every task and every assignment is becoming critical because everything is visible. Time is becoming more and more a scarce commodity.

- People are looking for reassurance that they are not wasting their time or their credibility and tend to look for a track record.

- Therefore, early winners are given more opportunities and early losers are given fewer second chances.

- As a result, early winners mature into proven winners and early losers often disappear into oblivion.

Note that this is a phenomenon that also happens between you and competitors:

- In sports, an early lead often gives you or your team a psychological advantage and may cause the opponent to give up.

- In business, a quick success may convince a potential competitor to not go against your line and focus instead on a more vulnerable opponent.

- In the animal world, the least fit antelope is the one who gets eaten first by the lions.

Economies of success could explain why optimists are typically more successful and why parties in a military conflict always seek to paint the outcome of any battle as a victory: building the perception that you are successful is a part of being successful!

****

About the Author

Elias Aractingi has logged more than 30 years of work experience spread on all six continents. Armed with a BBA from the American University of Beirut and an MBA from the Columbia University Graduate School of Business, he practiced banking in New York at Interaudi Bank and BSI-Banca della Svizzera Italiana before joining Booz&Co. in Singapore, Indonesia and Thailand for almost six years providing advice to the greatest institutions in the region, learning to derive concepts and rules from raw data and seeing patterns where others see random events. Moving to Lebanese banking giant BLOM Bank, Elias had a fruitful career building a world-class retail banking franchise and restructuring a number of entities. Based in Beirut, Elias also has a home in Miami, Florida.

208

www.ingramcontent.com/pod-product-compliance
Lightning Source LLC
Chambersburg PA
CBHW062041090426
42740CB00016B/2976